THE LIBRARY
ST. MARY'S COLLEGE OF MARYLAND
ST. MARY'S CITY, MARYLAND 20686

BLACK PERSPECTIVES ON CRIME AND THE CRIMINAL JUSTICE SYSTEM

A symposium sponsored by
The National Urban League

Edited by
Robert L. Woodson

With a preface by
Vernon E. Jordan, Jr.

G.K.HALL&CO.
70 LINCOLN STREET, BOSTON, MASS.

Copyright © 1977 by the National Urban League

Library of Congress Cataloging in Publication Data

Main entry under title:

Black perspectives on crime and the criminal justice
  system.

  Includes bibliographies and index.
  1. Crime and criminals—United States—
Congresses. 2. Criminal justice, Administration of
—United States—Congresses. 3. Racism—United
States—Congresses. I. Woodson, Robert L.
II. National Urban League.
HV6791.B55   364   77-12045
ISBN 0-8161-8039-3   2 - 14 - 79

This publication is printed on permanent/durable acid-free paper
MANUFACTURED IN THE UNITED STATES OF AMERICA

Table of Contents

iii

Foreword

When the National Urban League first began to consider convening a meeting of seven of the nation's leading black criminologists together with outstanding criminal justice practitioners, we were all very excited about the prospect of finally getting a different perspective on crime and how it affects the black community.

We were excited because we knew that black people constantly rank crime in their community among their most serious concerns. The Washington, D.C., Urban League recently conducted a survey of that community's residents and found that two of every three black citizens in low-income areas of that city said they walk in fear of neighborhood crime. And Washington residents are certainly not alone.

The first duty of any government is the safety and general welfare of its citizens. The widespread crime and fear that pervade black communities as night descends call into question the very stability of our political system.

Thus, crime has become a political issue. Often the call for "law and order" has been only a mask for racist demagoguery and has succeeded only in bringing crime into the national political arena.

We have watched as politicians and self-styled experts have sold the public on a "get tough" policy towards crime. Such a policy ignores the social causes of criminal behavior, treating racism, poverty, bad schools, and slum housing as irrelevant to the problem.

But we know that the social causes of crime are real. It is difficult to conceive of a crime-free society with large numbers of poor and unemployed, victimized by miseducation, forced into substandard housing, brutalized by racial discrimination. We know that crime will survive law and order campaigns as long as there are young people angered by rejection, inflamed by discrimination, and burdened by poverty.

Indeed, it is no coincidence that crime rose when two and a half million people were added to the poverty rolls in a single year and when 60 percent of black teenagers were out of work.

The criminologists and practitioners assembled for this symposium understand all of this. Thus, they bring a unique perspective on crime. They share with all black Americans a dual perspective. As victims of racial discrimination, blacks understand the forces that cause crime and feed criminal behavior. And as victims of crime, blacks are determined to combat both crime and the forces causing it.

Yet, the record shows that black people have been relentlessly excluded from active participation and policy making in anticrime efforts. And in large part, that is why the much publicized anticrime drives have failed.

It was our hope that this symposium will be a beginning of an inclusion of blacks into the criminal justice system.

VERNON E. JORDAN, JR.

Introduction

The "War on Crime" has been one of the few battles in our history in which the black community has not been recruited (conscripted?). Some years ago, the administration prematurely declared a victory in that war. But, then and now, on urban fronts throughout the country, thousands of poor and black people continue to be disproportionately victimized by crime. The lack of black participation in the fight against crime has created the false impression that the black community condones crime and protects criminals. Crime prevention, however, is a high priority in the black community. As the level of fear rises throughout the nation, minority organizations have asserted leadership with great energy in combating crime.

Various presidential commissions have recognized the importance of active citizen/community support in crime prevention. Yet, official attempts to introduce the "minority community perspective" into the criminal justice system have met with indifference, limited technical/funding support, and on occasion, open resistance. The Law Enforcement Assistance Administration (LEAA), established under the Omnibus Crime Control Act, 1968, as a vehicle for innovation, reform, and progress in the criminal justice system, has failed to recognize or support minority citizen involvement in the crime fight.

The Urban League has a particular interest in community participation in crime prevention—crime has ravaged the black community. The 17 percent increase in crime reported during 1975-1976 has been felt mainly in low-income and minority communities.

According to studies of victims of crime in thirteen American cities, blacks and other minorities are more than four times as likely to be victimized by crime as whites. Low and moderate income families experience significantly higher rates of robbery and aggravated assault. The studies also indicated that at least one-half of all crimes committed *are not* reported.

The criminal justice system should be the nation's first line of defense against crime. In minority communities, however, citizens must balance their concerns about escalating crime against their experiences with inequities and contradictions in the law enforcement system. The increasing numbers of poor and black people in correctional facilities appear to support the notion that wealth and race, rather than the extent of guilt or the nature of the crime, determine who goes to jail and for how long. The allocation of police resources and the responsiveness of law enforcement officials to preferred communities also appear to be subject to these same key determinants.

Although minorities are the most victimized by crime and the most penalized for criminal activity, they are the least represented in the staffing and management of our criminal justice system. In 1968, a study of twenty-eight police agencies by the National Advisory Commission on Civil Disorders found that in cities surveyed blacks amounted to 24 percent of the population, but only about 6 percent of the law enforcement personnel. Among the nearly 600,000 employees of state and local law enforcement agencies throughout the nation, only 21,000, or about 3.5 percent, are black. Despite some marked advances over the last decade, minority representation in professional staff levels of correctional institutions remains limited.

The quest for minority input extends beyond a desire for a "bigger piece of the pie." Despite the expenditure of $5 billion by the U.S. Department of Justice, new programs and research have failed to produce solutions to the crime problem. In many cases such research has proven to be anathema to the very communties they were designed to help.

One major metropolitan research institute operating over a three-year period with $2 million in LEAA funds has devised questionable community crime prevention plans. For example, this institute's solution to the high crime rate plaguing a neighborhood square involved fencing in the area. The recommendation, accompanied by an impressive array of supportive charts and documentation, was approved by city officials, though it had been developed with *no* input from area residents. If citizen protest is a measure of community involvement, then this project successfully involved the community. When citizens were appraised of the dubious "fencing" plan, they banded together in understandable opposition, and, after a heated debate with city officials, the plan was mercifully scrapped.

The institute also recommended changing street traffic patterns to reduce congestion in a residential-commercial neighborhood plagued with crime. The neighborhood included a number of small retailers and other commercial operations that would lose business with the change in traffic flow. The residents and merchants were not involved in the formation of this ill-devised plan, which, despite vigorous protests, was approved by the city. After all, the institute represented "experts" in the criminal justice field and served as the city's prime technical assistance resource. The citizens, however, documented the detrimental impact of the new traffic plan on the commerce of their area and initiated a lawsuit to halt it.

The Urban League takes the position that without the active involvement of blacks in programs, research, and policy, there can be no real war on crime.

Therefore, the League convened seven of this country's black criminologists, joined by outstanding criminal justice practitioners, lay community organizers, and ex-street gang members. The purpose was to gain insights and knowledge for the thoughtful design of alternatives for the black community to consider in its pursuit of secure neighborhoods.

This book includes those papers presented at the symposium along with the reactions by symposium participants and the two addresses given by luncheon speakers.

The guest speakers were Mr. Sterling Johnson, special drug prosecutor for the City of New York and Dr. James Q. Wilson, a leading sociologist and Professor of Government at Harvard University.

The systematic exclusion of blacks throughout the judicial process has resulted in the perpetuation of myths about black communities and of attacks upon them, and the depletion of their resources.

Black Perspectives on Crime and the Criminal Justice System has been brought to the American public in the hope that it will help illuminate the realities and the need for a holistic approach to crime in America.

Acknowledgments

Many individuals contributed to the success of the symposium. We would like to give special acknowledgement to a former staff member of the Administration of Justice Division, Ms. Johnsy Middleton, who assisted in organizing and coordinating the symposium. In addition, we would like to recognize Dr. Andrea Sullivan, who presented a paper on behalf of Dr. Julius Debro, who was out of the country at the time. Dr. Sullivan later joined the Urban League staff and provided valued help in editing the various papers. Other staff members who worked very diligently in assembling and typing materials included Wayman Young, Janie Ward, Ms. Sandra Satterwhite, Ms. Rosie Hernandez, and Ms. Jackie Sheppard, and special thanks to Ms. Renee DuJean for her consultation on the project.

The symposium was enriched by the participation of the various reactors representing a broad cross-section of the lay and criminal justice communities. Each person traveled at their own expense to the symposium from various cities throughout the country.

We would also like to thank the Carnegie Corporation and the New World Foundation whose support enabled this symposium to be held.

The Authors

JOHN O. BOONE Received the Masters in Psychiatric Social Work from Atlanta University and has done post-graduate work at the University of Chicago and the University of California. Mr. Boone is presently Director of Urban Affairs, WNAC-TV, RKO General Corporation, Boston, Massachusetts; and Director of the Campaign Against Prisons, Boston, Massachusetts. He is a member of the American Correctional Association, the National Council on Crime and Delinquency, and the National Council of Churches, Criminal Justice Program. Has worked extensively in correctional institutions and has served as a Senior Criminal Justice Fellow at the Boston University Law School, Center for Criminal Justice and at Harvard University Law School, Center for Criminal Justice. He has also taught at Boston University School of Social Work, Indiana State University and is presently a visiting professor at Clark University.

LEE P. BROWN, PH.D. Received the Master of Arts in Sociology from California State University and the Master and Doctorate in Criminology from the University of California at Berkeley. Dr. Brown is the Director of Justice Services in Multnomah County, Oregon. He is a former police officer and has taught at Howard University and Portland State University. He has published extensively in various professional journals. His memberships include the International Association of Chiefs of Police and the National Advisory Commission on Criminal Justice Standards and Goals.

BENJAMIN CARMICHAEL, PH.D. Received his Bachelor of Arts from San Francisco State College, Master of Arts and Doctor of Criminology degrees from the University of California, Berkeley. Dr. Carmichael is Associate Professor of Sociology at California State University, Hayward. He has taught at California State University, Hayward, University of San Francisco and University of California, Berkeley. His publications include "The Hunters Point Riot: Politics of the Frustrated" in *Issues in Criminology*. He is a member of the National Council on Crime and Delinquency.

JULIUS DEBRO, PH.D. Received the Master of Arts in Sociology from San Jose State College and the Doctorate of Criminology from the University of California, Berkeley. Dr. Debro is a Professor of Criminology of Maryland. He has taught at Laney College, Alameda College, the University of Maryland, and has conducted research on race relations in the Armed Forces. He is a member of the American Sociological Association, the Academy of Criminal Justice Sciences, American Society of Criminology and the National Council on Crime and Delinquency.

GEORGE NAPPER, PH.D. Received his Bachelor of Arts, Master of Criminology and Doctor of Criminology from the University of California, Berkeley. Presently, Dr. Napper is Director of the Crime Analysis Team, a Division of the Mayor's Office in Atlanta, Georgia. He has taught at Morris Brown College, Spelman College, Emory University, and the University of California, Berkeley. His publications include *Blacker Than Thou: The Struggle for Campus Unity*. He is a member of the Georgia State Crime Commission, Criminal Justice Coordinating Council, Atlanta, and the Board of Directors, American Civil Liberties Union of Georgia.

GWYNNE PEIRSON, PH.D., A.B.D. Received his Bachelor of Arts degree and the Master of Criminology degree from the University of California. He is due to receive his Ph.D. from the University of California in August, 1977. He is Assistant Professor of Criminology at Howard University. For 20 years, he was a police officer in Oakland, California. He has taught at the University of Missouri. His publications include *Police Operations*. He is a member of the American Sociological Association and the Academy of Criminal Justice Sciences.

ANDREA D. SULLIVAN, PH.D. (Presentor of Debro's Paper) Received her Bachelor of Arts degree from Cheyney State College, the Master of Arts in Criminology, and the Doctorate of Philosophy in sociology from the Center for Studies in Criminology and Criminal Law at the University of Pennsylvania. Dr. Sullivan is currently the Director of Crime Prevention at the National Urban League in New York City. She has taught at Howard University, American University and Federal City College. Her recent publication appears in *The Journal of Criminology*, November 1976, as a compelling critique of

Brownmiller's book, *Against Our Will: Men, Women and Rape.* She is a member of the American Society of Criminology, and the Association of Black Sociologists.

L. ALEX SWAN, PH.D., L.L.B. Received his undergraduate degree at the University of the West Indies. He pursued further studies at the University of London where he obtained a degree in legal aspects of business. He received a Master of Arts in Sociology from Atlanta University, and a Master and Ph.D. in Criminology at the University of California, Berkeley. He is Chairman of the Department and Professor of Sociology at Fisk University. He has taught at Tennessee State University, Vanderbilt University, Miami Dade Junior College and the University of California at Berkeley. His publications include *The Politics of Riot Behavior* and *Analysis of Selected Nations on Suicide.* He is a member of the Council on Crime and Delinquency, the American Society of Criminology and the American Sociological Association.

ROBERT L. WOODSON Received his Bachelors of Science degree from Cheyney State College and Masters of Social Work from the University of Pennsylvania. He is currently a fellow in residence at the American Enterprise Institute for Public Policy Research. He was formerly the Director of the Administration of Justice Department for the National Urban League. He was an adjunct professor at the New School for Social Research and Policy Analysis. He has taught at the Martin Luther King School for Social Change in Chester, Pennsylvania. His publications include "The Challenge of Black Power," *Trends* magazine; "Educational Policy and the Black Educators;" "The Relationship of the Law Enforcement Administration to the Black Community," a report by the National Urban League. Mr. Woodson is a member of the Board of Directors of the Center for Community Change, Board member of Offender Aid Restoration, and Consultant to the National Council of Juvenile Court Judges.

Opening Remarks

Welcome—*Dr. Ronald Davenport*

Overview of the Problem—*Robert L. Woodson*

Policy Formation and the Role of Black
Organizations—*Ronald Brown*

Robert Woodson: I'd like to outline for you the purpose of the conference and what we hope to accomplish, I think this will perhaps set the context in which we are gathered.

The National Urban League sees itself as a resource center, as a clearing house, as a point of reference in the whole area of criminal justice and in crime prevention, and to this end, we have engaged in a number of activities throughout the past four years. One of the principal activities has been the recruitment of minorities into the criminal justice system. We did this under contract with the Justice Department. We recruited actively in ten cities, recruiting about fifteen thousand minority people and placing over 6,000 in various law enforcement agencies. These included blacks, Chicanos, and native Americans, but were principally black people. Presently we are engaged in a study of crime and its control and prevention. We are trying to bring the resources of the black community to bear on this menacing problem. And to this end, I would like to just describe to you our strategy.

Our strategy is really in two parts. Under a grant from the Carnegie Corporation, we are able to assemble a staff of people who will collect data from various minority communities throughout this country, where people are actively engaged in the control and prevention of crime at the community level. We feel as though we have really not examined what the folks are doing out there; so that we can determine if there are common programmatic principles and themes.

So we're going to collect the data, analyze it, and draft a plan of action. We will expose this plan of action to a number of practitioners and social

1

scientists like yourselves, solicit your response and then incorporate this response into the crime prevention plan.

We hope to then establish some vehicle that will allow us to implement
programs based upon our findings, that are suitable for replication. We
hope to operate in approximately five or ten cities and demonstrate projects. To test these programmatic principles there will exist an exchange of
information between the field and central office, and then we hope to
make this information available to government, business and industry and
to black organizations.

We have established an advisory committee consisting of a number of
people, including ministers, criminal justice practitioners, and lay community folks. We hope to begin to forge an alliance which just does not exist in
the field at the present time, social scientists sitting down with people in the
community who are actually carrying out these programs.

This symposium is a part of the overall strategy and that is why we have
several aims in mind. One is to develop a body of data upon which criminal
justice practitioners like yourselves and others, can be guided in making policy
decisions.

Second, we wish to acquaint you with one another in hopes that through
shared experiences, you will begin to gain deeper insight and develop different approaches to solving the problem of crime.

And thirdly, we wish to acquaint the black community as well as the
American public with our social scientists so that when we meet with federal
and other officials, who commission research, we can point them in the
proper direction.

To this end, we hope that during these proceedings, that you will not
limit yourselves to just questions. We want to know about your experiences,
we want to know how you feel, what you think, what your notions are
about the problem, so that we can really have a rich experience.

Following this symposium, we will have all of your comments and those
of our scientists recorded and transcribed. It is our intention to produce a
book out of it, so that we can begin to share this with people throughout the
country.

Ronald Davenport: In the interim, while Bob was acquainting you
with the conference charge, we were joined by the new Deputy Director of
the Urban League, who also is in charge of our Washington Office, Mr.
Ron Brown. I think Mr. Brown would like to say a couple of words.

Ronald Brown: Thank you. Sorry for coming in in the middle
of Bob's remarks. I was asked to talk a little bit about public policy
and national black organizations, and I want to preface that with just a
few comments about the Urban League. Most of you around the room
are familiar with the league and what we do. Some of you may not be,

and I think it's important that we have that perspective as we start the day.

The Urban League has been around since 1910, involved initially with the problems of blacks as they moved from rural to urban areas and principally involved in economic development and job related problems. The scope of the league's activities has grown steadily over those years since 1910 to include a variety of social service delivery programs, and in recent years, we've been involved not only extensively in program and social service delivery, but also in strong advocacy programs in order to try to articulate the needs and aspirations of black people and other minority group people and poor people around the country.

I have a very personal interest in this program and in the efforts of Bob and all of you for a variety of reasons. About five or six years ago, I started the Administration of Justice Unit of the National Urban League and discovered Bob and brought him to the League. When I left that job, Bob took over and it has been through his leadership, with the help of people like Ron Davenport and many of you, that something like this has occurred today and that our efforts in the whole area of criminal justice, crime prevention and criminal justice system related issues have become a real priority, with the National Urban League. We hope to make these program efforts grow and prosper and I take a lot of personal pride in the kind of progress that has been made.

Just a word about public policy. First of all, I think you ought to understand a little something structurally about the Urban League. We're here at the National Urban League Headquarters in New York, along with this headquarters, there are four regional offices. There is also a Washington operation which has the Washington Bureau which I now direct, and a Research Department. There are also one hundred and five local Urban League affiliates scattered around the country, serving the needs of people at the local level.

I have been an advocate for many years of a much stronger position and posture on the part of not only the National Urban League, but black people and black organizations generally; the whole area of public policy formulation. It's been my thesis, that we ought to pay a good deal more attention to how we can have a significant impact on public policy in this country. An organization like the Urban League, even when put together with all of the other community organizations, cannot ever take over the work of the Police Department, and the work of social service delivery agencies of the government.

It seems to me that we have to be innovative, and that we have to be the people who can crystallize dynamic new social change concepts. People who can demonstrate program delivery in a way that program services have not been delivered, can assist in evaluating those programs and then assist in replicating them if they work.

It seems to me that this is an area, particularly in administration of justice, that we have not operated in our full capability in the past. I don't mean to tell you what the data shows, but principally we are dispropor- tionately represented among those who get caught up in the system, and virtually unrepresented among the decision makers in that system; although many of you around the room today certainly contradict that. I think if we look at the whole picture, we will see that our representation among decision makers in the area is virtually nil.

We must find ways to do something about that, we must find ways to focus attention on making systemic changes. How can our program concept be turned into things that then have impact on major public policy deter- minations in this country? As I indicated, we can't run a program or a project that's gonna reach everybody that has a need. What we can do is run a program or a project that demonstrates the need for some systemic change, which gives us the data base so that we can then become strong advocates for change in the system, as it relates to those folks that we're most concerned about.

And it really seems to me that it is bringing you together and it is also helping us in formulating these new creative concepts in the area of admin- istration of justice.

So I hope as we go about, we can think not only in terms of programs and projects that are an end in and of themselves, but in my judgement they should never be. They should create a product, they should create a data base, they should create group incentive experiences which allow us to learn and grow, and then take that experience and turn it into something that can then be used by everyone. It can become a part of that system's change agent that we wish to be. And I hope, that as we go about our deliberation, we can keep in mind the broader picture and the broader concern about how we can maximize our influence and how we can indeed have the maximum impact on that system that we think so desperately needs changing.

Perception of Crime:
Problems and Implications

by George Napper

One of the most formidable problems facing American society today is crime. Crime is not a new phenomenon and indeed has been characterized by some as "an American way of life." What is new about crime is that it is only now beginning to be scrutinized by the masses of people because of its growth and complexity, its destructive effects on national life and its psychologically, socially and economically damaging effects.

Violent crimes, so-called "street crimes," are particularly feared. It is the belief of many that such crimes "threaten the very existence of a humane and civilized society" and thus should receive foremost attention. Justification for focusing upon these crimes may be found in the nation-wide statistics on them. Most recent FBI statistics show the murder rate to be 9.7 per 100,000; robbery, 208.8/100,000; burglary, 1429/100,000; and larceny, 2473/100,000 to name a few.

Reports indicate that shoplifting losses frequently eat up 1 to 5 percent of merchants' sales; the costs of crime attributable to drug abuse is $5 billion; and one burglar apprehended in a large mid-western city admitted stealing $200,000 worth of property.

Astounding as these figures may seem, that crime which has been most overlooked has even greater economic costs. The President's Commission on Law Enforcement and Administration of Justice concluded that the income realized from organized crime is almost double the amount other criminals derive from all other forms of criminal activity combined.

When lifestyles are altered as a result of crime, when the high level of violence causes cities and homes to become "armed camps," and when fear of criminal victimization grips even residents of rural communities, the end result is the disfigurement of society and downgrading of the quality of life.

If questioned then, most Americans would readily agree that crime is a great plague facing our society. They would maintain that criminal behavior

5

is abnormal, they would vehemently denounce it, and would express great concern and fear of it. There appears to be little question that crime is a social problem, violative of the cultural norms and collective conscience of society.

Lawyers, judges, criminologists and others have developed various concepts of crime and criminality in an effort to explain and contend with this problem. Yet, the fundamental questions of "what is crime" and "who are the criminals" have yet to be satisfactorily answered.

Highly emotional public reaction to crime and criminals has tended to cloud our understanding. However, clarity of understanding as to the nature of the problem is a prerequisite to dealing with it effectively.

The legal conceptualization of criminal behavior is that behavior which is in violation of the criminal law, although widely accepted, fails to convey the full meaning which it has come to have. Such definitions are precise and exact but are deceptive in that the substance of law is fluid, continually yielding to societal pressure and changed perceptions and standards of conduct.

Criminologists have developed several schools of thought which attempt to explain crime and criminal behavior.

The traditional classical school contended that, through the exercise of his free-will, man could make conscious decisions. Thus, if one made the conscious choice to commit crime, then his punishment is justified.

A basic assumption of this view is that forces within the individual are the greatest determinant of whether or not he will engage in criminal behavior. Any struggle or conflict regarding the morality or legality of certain acts will be thrashed out, in consultation with expectations of reward or punishment, before a deliberate choice is made. The impacts and pressures of social factors in influencing individual behavior receive virtually no attention under this school of thought.

The basic tenet of the positivist school of thought is that the "criminal" is a being who is pushed by forces over which he has very little control. Crime causation is "blamed" on the genetic, the biological, the psychological and/or the physical makeup of the individual who is viewed as different from the "non-criminals."

This orientation differs from the classical school in that it assumes that no rational, normal person would deliberately violate the norms of society. Anyone who does so violates such norms because he cannot help himself.

Other theories have attempted to explain causality and develop solutions to this social problem. Freud's psychological focus held that man's thoughts and emotions impacted upon his behavior, while Karl Marx believed that the destruction of capitalism and social classes would wipe out crime.

These explanations of crime and criminals, with the exception of Marx's theory, tend to discount the importance of those elements of modern society which impinge upon man's behavior. Precise, narrow and changeless definitions of crime are assumed. Also implied in these schools of thought is the belief that the "criminal" is somehow qualitatively different than the noncriminal. Either evilness or biological defectiveness would lead to a violation of the norms of society.

The deficiencies of existing theories of crime have led to the development in this paper of a radical approach. The ideas which are presented attempt to extend the conceptualization of crime beyond narrow definitions by embracing the factors of white collar crime, and struggles between various groups and social classes.

For all practical purposes, the prevailing ideas reflect a belief that crime and criminal behavior are inherent to particular racial/ethnic and economic groups.

Some observers of the problem have concluded that:

> The definition of crime in the first instance is found on the statute books, but it is highly modified, sometimes to the point of extinction by both administrative (police and prosecutorial) action and by judicial interpretation.

The modification of definitions of crime is also given form, direction and impetus by certain interest groups within society. This contention calls for an examination of what the modified definitions of crime are and the extent of such modifications. This is necessary because the consequences are such that certain status groups receive differential treatment. This action, in turn, deflects attention away from the true issues which must necessarily be dealt with before the crime problem can be brought under control. This paper attempts such an examination.

A few months ago I was reading an article, that discussed the role that myths play in shaping the cruelty with which man frequently treats animals. The article focused on the situation of wolves to illustrate its point. It indicated that for years it has been believed that wolves roam about in packs and viciously attack unarmed humans, especially infants and women.

This particular situation, the article continued, was indicative of the kinds of problems that early Americans met as they were making their way west. The myth existed in spite of the fact that few, if any, cases of wolves threatening innocent human beings have ever been recorded in this part of the continent.

The main point of the article was that the existence of this myth, the perception of wolves in these terms allowed—indeed gave a license to—man to kill wolves for sport, pelts or simple vindictiveness.

It is difficult for me to avoid seeing the parallels between man's perception of wolves and the ensuing action; and society's perception of crime and criminality and the impact of that perception on how we have dealt with these issues in this society. In fashioning myths about crime and criminality experts have: 1) selectively chosen from an abundance of evidence and information that data which highlights black participation in the criminal arena; 2) used and continue to use that very special piece of data as the basis for making an ultimate statement of the truth and reality of crime this country; 3) cultivated an environment, through the press and other forms of mass media, those aspects of the spectrum of crime that tend to give support to the belief that blackness and criminality are synonymous terms; and thus 4) aggravated the crime problem by breeding distrust and disrespect in one sector of the community, while protecting the criminality in another sector of the community through a policy of benign neglect and leniency.

Perhaps another way of stating the above is to say that the drama of black crime and criminality in this country unfolds itself with the context of a "self-fulfilling prophecy." Much of what we think and feel about crime and the black community is unrelentingly and inextricably interwoven with this concept. Perceptions and preconceptions of criminals as being blacks become reality because those aspects of reality that support the belief are officially recognized and dramatized. The reactions of significant institutions in our society respond and react to these perceptions in ways as to sustain such views.

I contend that as long as the nature of the crime problem is confused with the group of people who have been officially, but erroneously, identified with it, we can only expect, at best, a shadowboxing with the symptoms rather than a meaningful attempt to fight the root causes of crime.

I have no intention of downgrading or in any way minimizing the importance of our coming to grips with the ugly octopus of crime, whose tentacles touch all of us in some way. I am, however, concerned that the nature of the reactions—given to our perception of the criminal—not be a worse problem than crime itself. This is a very critical concern that is not without some basis.

The impact of such perceptions was brought forth forcefully when the Omnibus Crime Control and Safe Streets bill was before the Congress as a response to the crime problem. Title II of the bill allowed for the taking of a confession without a lawyer's presence, allowed for detention of suspects without prompt arraignment, called for suspending the Writ of *Habeas Corpus* for those who had been previously convicted of a crime, and allowed wiretapping.

Title I of the bill provided for massive financial assistance to local police departments. The 1964 Civil Rights Act explicitly prohibited federal support to any agency engaged in racial discrimination. The pending bill nullified that rule as it regards police departments; it stated that they were not required to show a quota system or racial balance in order to receive aid. The bill would have prevented the government from supporting the 1964 act.

The bill's appeal was that it would provide a very valuable aid to crime fighting. The bill's supporters justified its unconstitutionality by saying certain measures would be used only against "known criminals." But who is a "criminal?" Think about that question for a moment, for I will later raise it again. Presumably after a person has paid his debt to society by serving out his sentence, he is legally no longer a criminal. The term "criminal" legally refers only to people in jail or on parole. But the spirit of the bill was that anyone suspected of wrongdoing would be considered a criminal and could be treated according to the bill's provisions.

The provisions of the bill required us to trust the discretionary powers of the police and to believe that they would not abuse such powers. The police would decide who is and who is not a criminal. The Fifth Amendment through the due process clause, acknowledges that the writers of the Constitution did not have such faith, and history has demonstrated that there is no reason for low and middle income Americans to have such faith either. While many of the ominous provisions of the bill were not passed, it does suggest the kind of mentality that can and does appear when it is time to do something about crime and our manufactured criminal. The frightening implications of having such provisions in a democratic society are very apparent and need no elaboration.

A moment ago I raised the question "Who is a criminal?" I am quite sure that you have come up with several definitions. But whatever those definitions are, I am sure that for the most part they exclude any reference to yourself as being a criminal. Perhaps your conclusions are justifiable. I would imagine that many of you have concluded that a criminal is somehow a different kind of person than you are. Someone who is qualitatively different; someone who can be dismissed as a non-person and who is, therefore, rightfully deserving of any and all kinds of negative treatment he receives. Certainly, if criminals become defined as non-persons, objects, animals, then the kinds of social policies and strategies we put together to deal with him will reflect such an attitude. Perhaps this is why many of us have very little real concern about the conditions that characterize prison life; about what happens to those who are released from prison and try to establish or re-establish ties with the conventional world. Indeed, because too many of our citizens have characterized those who inhabit the ghettos, the barrios and the reservations as immoral, evil and nasty. We expect them to do immoral things. "That's the way they are" becomes a justification for doing nothing about the objective material conditions of their lives, and a justification for not seeing them as part of the human family.

Let us, for the sake of discussion, define a criminal as one who has committed an act that is in violation of a criminal law. An interesting exercise that I have performed on occasions when I have taught a criminology course is to ask each of the students to write down on a piece of paper five or six acts that he has committed in violation of the law. Then I collect the pieces of paper and read back to them what they have written down. It sounds like a lightweight roll call in San Quentin! I would imagine that a similar exercise done here would produce the same results notwithstanding the fact that you are among the leading citizens of the city and that it has never occurred to you that you have as much in common behaviorally speaking with people in state prisons as you have with the good people who presently sit on either side of you. Perhaps, what become clear here is that there is no qualitative difference between those of us here and many people sitting in prisons at this moment. No one is intrinsically criminal; criminality is a label applied by individuals with the power to do so.

How is it then that some people are selected for differential treatment and others are not, if all of us have been involved in generally similar types of behavior? It is apparent that criminal status may be ascribed to persons because of real or imagined attributes, because of what and who they are, rather than what they do, and justified by reference to real or fabricated behavior. Let us cite a couple of examples that have appeared over the years:

A. The Marijuana Situation—a law that is violated by many people allows the police to choose certain ones to punish for violation. The law making possession of marijuana a felony is such a law. For the majority of offenders, the law was not enforced. The police can pick out whom they want to punish. Usually, these people are picked out because they are annoying to legal authorities for some other reason such as the way they walk, clothes they wear, etc.

B. Gun Laws: Another tactic is to dig up an old law. For example, a few years back Bobby Seale was convicted of violating an old law, one against carrying a gun near a jail, which had not been enforced for years. Clearly, he was wanted for reasons other than this "crime."

C. Another example takes us even further back and is related to the late Congressman Adam Clayton Powell. The original reason for the suit against Powell which eventually led to his eviction from Congress was that he called a woman a "windy old bag-woman." Some of you might recall when President Truman called the columnist Drew Pearson "a son of a bitch" because he made unkind remarks about the President's daughter's singing ability. Yet no one would think of suing Truman. We must say that the law is misused when it is applied to some persons and not others.

While the above cases are noteworthy examples of the unequal application of the law, it is the collective impact of selective treatment on crime statistics, how such statistics influence and distort our understanding of crime and criminality; and the implications for the black community that I now wish to turn my attention to.

UNIFORM CRIME REPORT

The entire public dialogue about crime, crime waves, criminality and law and order is almost wholly based on crime statistics gathered by the FBI and issued annually as the Uniform Crime Report (UCR). Usually the contents of the report provide ammunition to the police lobbyists and rightwing extremists who scream that the Supreme Court had coddled criminals and urge the need to support one's local police. More important, the contents of the report compel one to understand why criminality and blackness are perceived as synonymous terms.

If one is told that an overwhelming proportion of people who are arrested are black and that the population of the jails and prisons on our country are predominantly and increasingly drawn from the black community, one is forced to conclude that the argument suggesting that blackness and criminality can be used interchangeably has merit. So profound is the connection that it is extremely difficult to find someone—black or white—who will fail to conjure up images of a black male when asked to provide the portrait of a criminal.

William Ryan (*Blaming the Victim*) tells us that there are at least two basic problems with the UCR that we ought to be aware of. First he states that the UCR is a gross underestimation of the actual crime rate. He cites a survey taken by the President's Crime Commission showing that by the most conservative standards the actual crime rate is at least double or triple the rate reported by the FBI.

In terms of the focus on this paper, the second problem that Ryan identifies is the more important one. He points out the UCR does not take into consideration the phenomena of organized crime and white collar crime. Organized crime scarcely gets counted in crime statistics despite the fact that its actual yield in profits is in the billions of dollars.

As to white collar crime, it is normally not even counted as crime, even when it is specifically known to officials. White collar crime is crime committed by business and professional people in the course of their occupations. A physician who commits an illegal abortion, falsifies a prescription for a drug addict, or pads a bill; or a businessman who systematically short-weights his product, misbrands it, embezzles the firm's funds, manipulates a phony bankruptcy or falsifies his financial statement in violation of state and federal laws which regulate business conduct are examples of what we mean by white collar crime. Despite the fact that such acts are punishable by law, attitudes toward white collar crime contrast sharply with the public indignation at conventional crime. To most people many forms of white collar crime are not viewed as being "real crimes." They are not viewed as genuine crime either by the public or by the perpetrators.

It is of interest to note the relative absence of a punitive response to the local banker who embezzles a million dollars from the bank. The outcry, if there is any, is aimed at protecting the person from going to prison by making claims that he is an outstanding citizen because of big donations to the Boy Scouts and the YMCA, etc.

The exclusion of organized criminal activities and white collar activities from UCR drastically underestimates the amount of crime taking place in this country. Another effect of this highly selective mode of recording criminality is to paint a false picture of who or what the criminal is. Such recording leads to a distortion of what crime is all about.

The official picture counts those kinds of behavior that just happen to be peculiar to certain groups. Hartjen speaks of those implications of selective counting:

> The middle-class executive, for example, is not likely to commit burglary. He doesn't need to. But price fixing is within his realm of possibility. Laws restricting this kind of conduct exist—true. They are, however, loosely formulated and seldom enforced—not only because it is difficult to do so. The frequency of this conduct may actually be much higher than that of burglary or other forms of conduct typical of the powerless classes. But it is rarely noticed or counted. One can wonder why. Indeed, one can only imagine what patterns would appear in crime rates were the powerless able to determine what is to be recorded. But then they would no longer be powerless.

Thus the official picture minimizes and deflects attention away from one kind of crime. By omitting categories of crime that are overwhelmingly dominated by white participants and singling out categories disproportionately shared by blacks, we have an official picture that does three things: 1) It makes it difficult to keep images of black people from coming to one's mind when the issue of crime is raised; 2) makes blackness synonymous with criminality by definition; 3) sets the stage for a quality of response to crime that is based on a division of people into two classes, the good and the bad. This unrealistic image has the effect of reinforcing the myth that only evil, bad and crazy people commit crimes.

GOOD PEOPLE AND BAD PEOPLE

Duster, in his book *The Legislation of Morality,* makes the point that certain social categories lend themselves more to moral condemnation than others. That moral hostility comes faster and easier when directed toward a young, lower-class black male, than toward a middle-aged, middle-class person. He takes the case of addiction to drugs to demonstrate the dramatic social difference it makes whether the finger of moral indignation is pointed by or at the middle class.

Duster shows that at the turn of the century anyone could go to a corner druggist and buy grams of morphine or heroin for just a few pennies just as we now go to buy aspirins. No prescription was needed. Because of the fact that the middle and upper classes were the overwhelming consumers, there was no moral stigma attached to narcotics use. People who were addicted were viewed in basically the same terms we view diabetics today. We say that is too bad but they are not ostracized from conventional circles or held in disrespect. But as social conditions were altered and drug usage became a phenomena increasingly associated with young lower class blacks, the kind of language used to define the new users indicated a moral reassessment of what had previously been regarded as a physiological problem. While in the earlier period the physiology problem was thought of first, we now conceive of today's user as "an immoral, weak, psychologically inadequate criminal who preys upon an unsuspecting population to supply his 'morbid' appetite." Along with the re-definition, the penalties under law also underwent drastic transformation. From a point where there were no regulations to date for sale to minors (in 1956 with the passing of the Narcotic Drug Control Act by Congress) to some states where being an addict is a crime.

The marijuana experience is very similar to the opiate experience although the direction of change was in reverse of the heroin problem. As long as marijuana use was viewed as an experience peculiar to the black lower class, it was defined as being a bad, nasty, evil habit engaged in by people who are defined as bad, nasty and evil. The laws were punitive. However, when it became apparent that marijuana was increasingly becoming a part of the lifestyle of the middle class community, society was placed in a dilemma. Should it re-define the good people engaged in smoking marijuana as bad, evil, nasty people; or should it re-define what had been characterized as a bad and evil habit as being an acceptable habit? It is very clear what the decision is.

Duster would respond to the above phenomena by saying: "When it is part of the public view that the predominant perpetrators of the act come from the moral center, the act cannot long remain 'immoral' or deviant; it can become deviant again only under circumstances where the public conception is that the 'morally susceptible' classes are those who are the primary indulgers."

Duster's analysis aids us in understanding the difficulty in perceiving white collar crimes on the same moral level as conventional crime—the white community on the same moral plane as the black community; or the upper and middle classes on the same level as lower classes.

Yet when the final count is in, regarding the actual picture of criminal activity, it is clear that blacks and the lower class have no monopoly on crime. Whites are, if not more involved, just as involved in criminal activities as blacks are. Indeed, if a monetary value were placed on the profits derived from the various categories of crime where either group is disproportionately involved, street crime would be nothing more than a drop in the sea of criminal activity characterized by white collar crime and organized crime.

The kinds of crimes committed by members of the social groups being discussed here are compatible with their position in the social structure. Unemployed people cannot, by definition, commit white collar crimes. Middle class executives and professionals have no need to commit such crimes as robbery and burglary when they can fix prices or embezzle money.

There is no qualitative difference between the two types of perpetrators. Their relative positions in the social structure dictate the kinds of instruments used to achieve their ends. *One is able to use the pen; the other has to use the gun.* If the latter thought he could achieve his ends without the gun, he would. It the former had to use the gun to avoid detection, he would.

The real difference lies, of course, in the political arena. One group has the power to make rules and to single out for differential treatment those who are defined as being different, powerless and morally susceptible.

Everyone knows, blacks especially, that Sutherland was correct when he said that 1) upper class persons who commit crimes are frequently able to escape arrest and conviction because their money and social position make them more powerful politically; and 2) laws that apply exclusively to business and the professions, and which therefore involve only upper class people, are seldom dealt with by criminal courts. And, of course, everyone knows that people who commit traditional crimes are dealt with far more harshly than those who commit white collar crimes.

In a case involving the Sherman Anti-trust Act, the executives of seven electrical manufacturing corporations were convicted of a price conspiracy involving over one billion dollars and sentenced to thirty days in jail each. Meanwhile, seemingly sadistic sentences were meted out to poor people convicted of crimes in the streets. A man in Ashbury Park, N. J., for instance, was convicted of stealing a $2.98 pair of sunglasses and a dollar box of soap. He was sent to jail for four months. Joseph Sills in Dallas, Texas, was sentenced to 1,000 years in prison for stealing $73.10. George Jackson spent ten years in prison for driving the getaway car in a robbery involving $70.00. The list goes on and on. These are just a few illustrations of the severity of the criminal justice system when applied to poor people.

It is apparent to me that if any meaningful inroads are to be made in controlling the problem of crime in the black community, the differential law enforcement activities that is endemic to the criminal justice system has to be alleviated. It is not only blatantly unfair, but it is increasingly difficult for minority communities to accept a criminal justice system that is lenient towards and protects the criminality of one sector while being severe and over-dramatizing the criminality of another sector of the community. The implications for a growing disrespect for the law and for law enforcement personnel is all too obvious.

Thus, there is a need to correct the crime picture so that the citizens of this country can begin to perceive correctly what crime and criminality are all about. The *Uniform Crime Report* is not only an obstacle to this goal, it 1) blatantly generates false perceptions of crime; and 2) provides the basis for believing that criminality is synonymous with blackness.

The above situation not only fans the flames of racism; it also aggravates the crime problem by breeding and heightening distrust and disrespect of the law in communities already having more than their share of problems; while indulging and shielding the criminality of the upper circles of our society.

RE-DEFINING CRIME

A basic belief shared by many residents of the black community is that the government has the responsibility to provide its citizens with the opportunities to acquire the basic necessities of life. In turn, the citizens will comply with the rules and laws established by the government. This is referred to as the social contract theory. When the government fails to uphold its end of the bargain, citizens do not feel a total obligation to obey the rules and laws.

The problem of not providing the basic necessities is not only a serious one, it also raises, on its own terms, some important questions about what crime is really all about.

I contend that the compelling argument presented by Herman and Julia Schwendinger provides a very important perspective in defining crime or expanding upon the present legal definition.

They suggest that we need a definition of crime that moves away from the preservation of a social order that is built on inequality; that moves away from protecting those engaged in sustaining conditions of inequality and human misery.

We need a definition that says crime is a violation of basic human rights—the right to decent food, shelter and human dignity. Under this definition any individual who is engaged in denying these rights is a criminal;

and any situation or condition which causes the abrogation of these rights would be seen as criminal.

Re-defining crime along such lines would, among other things, reduce some of the academic craze over such issues as whether or not poverty causes crime; since poverty itself would be viewed as criminal.

Finally, it is only by making the objective social conditions under which people live the target of social policy that the most significant intrusions on the problem of crime on the black community can be achieved. The unwillingness to bring the resources of this country to bear upon the negative social conditions that too frequently characterize the ghettos, the barrios and the reservations not only constitutes a form of social entrapment but also helps guarantee that new generations of youngsters will find their way into society's records of criminal statistics.

REACTION

Davenport: Crime has been defined as reaching certain kinds of anti-social conduct which are engaged in by economic classes. If you redefine this to mean something else, crime would change. There is such a thing as anti-social conduct; there are people who belong in jail. To what extent can we as black folk or we as Mexican Americans or we as the economically lower classed in this society, begin to isolate those people who are part of our community and who do commit anti-social acts. I mean like a purse-snatching, like a rape, like a robbery?

Napper: There's a need for some other kinds of things to take place first. The way in which crime is perceived and defined has a lot to do with the particular policies that are generated. I'm not trying to minimize the extent to which crime exists in black communities, but what I'm concerned about here is providing the conditions under which we can properly view what the entire criminal picture is all about. When we can do that and give others, people other than black people their rightful share of responsibility and blame for crime, then I think we can expect more humane kinds of social policies to emanate from those who are the movers and shakers of society.

Davenport: You're taking a traditional liberal role, the problem is that we don't define crime properly to include all the folks who commit anti-social acts, and I would agree with that generally speaking. But that doesn't deal with the problem. That doesn't deal with it on a kind of day-to-day basis.

Swan: I think what is important to understand is that although what has been presented may not deal with the entire issue, it does focus on the relationship of the definition of crime to the nature of the society. I'm suggesting, that we are not going to deal effectively with the problem of crime, when it's in the black community, until we deal with the central capitalist colonial nature of the American society. It is my understanding, after looking at the society, that it needs the definition. It needs that definition of the colonized being the bad people or the oppressed being the bad people. It needs that for its survival, thus it needs crime. This society, this capitalist colonial society could not exist without crime.

Even though the definition may assist us, it will not impact the nature of crime until we understand the nature of what I call the capitalist colonial society; its need for powerless people and its need for blaming those oppressed powerless people for the rate of crime in this society. If we're going to effectively impact the nature of crime in American society, whether it is white collar or what have you, then we have to talk about the structure of the American society. We need to look at the system, meaning the political arrangements, the economic arrangements, the educational and legal arrangements. For instance, let's look at vagrancy laws; the vagrancy law came into existence after 1863, when black folks just hung around saying, I don't want to go back on the plantation. The plantation owner said now how can we get these folks back on the plantation? They're messing up our economic situation. They said you just cannot hang around no more. They arrested us or put us in jail and then hired us to the plantation owners. I'm saying the nature of that kind of arrangement needs to be changed, although I agree that the definition is important too. But the very nature of the society must be changed. Yes sir.

Carmichael: I would simply add that George has identified the problem at two levels. One is a definitional issue, defining crime, defining who the criminal is. The other questions are much more programmatical. It involves law enforcement, and restructuring of resources in the larger communities. So that on one hand, we're defining or we're opening up our definition of crime, and secondly, we need to speak to those kinds of strategies that might be undertaken to address the particular problem of crime in communities.

Napper: I like to elaborate just a little bit on what Ben is saying. It seems to me that it is very difficult to determine the proper strategy in the absence of a clear definition of what the problem is.

Now we all might agree that there are individuals who need to go to jail. But there is no guarantee that taking that individual out of that situation, if we assume that there's some relationship between the present conditions and criminal behavior, is going to alleviate the problem. Family and social ties coupled with a difficult re-entry, the likelihood of that person becoming involved is eminent. So this individualized approach to the crime situation which I think has been suggested here is not the answer. Further it is very clear to me that society accepts white collar crime. Maybe we ought to be concerned about getting our people into situations where they can commit white collar crime if they're going to commit any crime at all. So that at least that becomes acceptable. You know, people talk about changing the prison system. Now an honest person would say well, the best way to change the prison system is to get a new class of prisoners. It will change a prison. You build new prisons that are just like the colleges for the white collar criminals, look at the Watergate people, and where they were sent is better than the residential area where I live. Right? So perhaps some of those people committing street crimes should be sent to prison where the conventional criminals are.

So I think this is very fundamental in terms of developing the proper strategy to deal with the whole issue of crime. I'm not sure that the strategies which have been put together, which, have been fashioned so far, have done anything to significantly reduce crime. I think because of this particular definition of what crime is all about; it's blackness—that's what it means.

Carmichael: I think also, that the notion of the self-fulfilling prophecy that Dr. Napper made is very important here. If you define crime in black terms, then you accord more money, more law enforcement personnel to enforce the law against black people, and this affects the rate of crime. If you have more people addressing crime in a particular community, then the crime rate in that community begins to rise.

Sulton: The definitions of crime cause certain reactions, behavioral reactions both at the level of the "criminal community" and the so-called law enforcement community. Before we can really get to any kind of strategy, we have to focus in on particular communities and the kinds of behavior, the kinds of social structure and economic opportunities that exist in those communities rather than try to deal with a national level piece of legislation to redefine crime.

The question, the problem with that is that legislation comes through power and the people who are in favor of the redefinition are not the persons that have the power to legislate. So I tend again to focus down on the community level where the impact I think will be very meaningful.

Ward: The idea that crime is just really defined in racial terms is a little bit, I think, simplistic. If you look at New York State prisoners in correctional institutions fifty, sixty years ago, they were white, at that time. The churches that are in New York State correctional facilities are Catholic churches or synagogues.

Napper: I'm simply saying that placed in an either/or situation, the programmatic approach lacks meaning unless you put it in the proper perspective. We should try to provide a picture that I think puts crime in a proper perspective if we anticipate any kind of meaningful programs to deal with the whole issue of crime.

Murray: I think we can uncouple the assumption of blackness and crime being synonymous if we just simply look at the things historically for the last hundred years or so, it's the poor in urban areas of this country who have filled the prisons, and the ones who have been finding their conduct being designated as crime by those who write the statutes.

Assume that, for the moment, it is probably going to continue for some time, you are involved in the structure in Atlanta. Assuming that you could make the determination about the reallocation of resources in Atlanta to deal with the problem, and conceding that you feel that there is a greater need to attend to the problems of organized and white collar crime, how would you go about reallocating those resources in Atlanta to bring about some kind of change in the ways things exist and bring about some sort of improvement in living conditions there?

Napper: We need more leadership that says problems like infant mortality rate, problems of unemployment and some other kinds of things that are endemic to the ghettos are gonna be dealt with. This is a priority. To stand up and say that we are concerned about your well being, and we're gonna pump moneys into dealing with that. To me that is terribly important. It seems a very small thing to do, but I have not seen that kind of leadership exercised in any of these major cities, where moneys would be committed, on a priority basis, in dealing with those kinds of problems. Those problems that I consider to be criminal. And I think that's very important in terms of getting people in the cities committed to what the city is all about. And as long as there's an absence of that kind of leadership, you know, it's easy for me to understand why people say well the hell with the mayor, or the hell with the governor, you know, I'm gonna go out and I'm gonna hustle and I'm gonna survive the best way I can. I have no obligation to the rules and laws of this community because apparently the community has no obligation to my situation. To me that's the key.

Davenport: Are you suggesting that because a banker goes free from embezzlement or the GE trust fixers get thirty days in jail, that somebody else is gonna knock somebody over the head?

Napper: I'm saying that has implications for how people in the other parts of the community view the whole situation of crime. I think it's a negative year.

Lamb: I get from Dr. Napper's remarks also the very clear message to the degree that the power or powerless is very much involved, and particularly, I think this relates to what Dr. Swan said earlier in reference to certain parts of the country being colonized or very much influenced and directed by others who are absentee or whatever. I'm wondering what the relationship would be between community involvement and the matter of selective enforcement. Selective enforcement, I think is very much the backbone of UCR or whatever definitions take place. To what extent are efforts being made to involve communities at the local level in the decision making process as it pertains to selective enforcement?

Brown: Well, that really was what my remarks were directed to, that until we are able to use that community experience and that desire that people have at the local level to have input into that process, we're not gonna be able to make an effective argument for making the kind of policy changes that we need to make.

So my suggestion really was that I guess the people that are gathered here to make the point more clearly than I can make it and that is that. In past years we have not had access to one another so we have been fighting for this access. Now we have begun to achieve some access and in my judgment, we have not yet effectively used that access. The League is therefore what we are trying to formulate a way in which we can now use the access to one another to have impact on policy. The only way to effectively do that is to use our project and program experiences which are by and of themselves, by definition, community approaches. To use those approaches, to gain from them community participation, the kind of data, information and knowledge which would allow us to then deal effectively with public policy issues.

We are dealing with a political problem, and I think that once we understand and recognize that, that our approach, our solutions, and our strategies should be predicated upon that knowledge.

Sullivan: What we're talking about clearly is power. No act in and of itself is a crime. There are acts that are labelled as criminal by persons who are in power, who believe that act to be socially harmful to whatever their needs or interests are. We must begin to think about getting into those positions, or either influencing persons who are already in those positions. We have to develop certain images, self-images. We don't have to look to the white man to present images of what we're supposed to be, according to his standards.

Davenport: What would you do tomorrow assuming that resources were not a problem?

Lamb: I think one of the things that you'd have to do would be to provide resources and disseminate information as much as possible so that people who are very much impacted by crime can understand how the system functions both on a formal and an informal basis. Community groups must be assisted in identifying the leverage and the fulcrums that they would need to impact on selective enforcement. The education of the community should be first.

Napper: I think in a nutshell, by redefining crime to include the kinds of things I talked about, you may not tomorrow change the behavior of people in any community, all right? But I think that ultimately, when people understand that whites and others are as criminal as blacks, moneys will come for community programs, highly influenced by that perception. As long as crime is viewed in terms of blackness, there are not going to be resources coming to communities to alleviate the kinds of problems that attend these communities.

Swan: For instance, this society is based on the philosophical principle of dog eat dog, as opposed to what I have come to look at as an African philosophical principle of the survival of the tribe; the oneness of being. Our society is the kind of capitalist society irrespective of the redefinition of criminal behavior, irrespective of whatever programs, that would generate the kind of crime that it needs. It needs powerless people like police need arrests and psychiatrists need sick folk. They generate these people; they institute those problems day after day to legitimize their efforts.

Ward: I'm here to represent the meanwhile things, the white collar crime. All of the white collar acts are now criminal by definition. There is no need to redefine them, they are already defined as criminal. The difference lies in the people in power: Their decision to prosecute against this kind of behavior or to do nothing about it. When they do, they come out with a probation as the final disposition, and even when you get a U.S. attorney as we have in the Southern District here in New York now, who has decided to cut in on white collar crime he finds that he has no law enforcement arm that can enforce that.

One final point, to make Archie's point again, is that there are no unlimited dollars. Almost all of the dollars that are ever going to be available are available now and it's not LEAA, that's only a drop in the bucket, it's municipal dollars that are the dollars in fighting criminality, and those municipal dollars are directed by those people who control those agencies, and if it's a Dr. Lee Brown controlling it, that's one kind of direction that we'll give or Reginald Eaves. If we don't put those people in those positions, you will not get those changes of policy. It must come fron that end. It must come from community and practitioners in control.

Napper: We must concern ourselves with those kinds of conditions that relate directly to much of the criminality that black people are involved in. The thrust of all my remarks is to suggest that I think a redefinition of crime has to look at those conditions that attend the reality of black existence as being a criminal kind of circumstance. That should be the target of social policy, and not the individual, even if the individual is going to be radically changed, as an individual, that still does not deal with the conditions under which he was raised.

The Muslims have been very effective in certain kinds of ways, in terms of changing the world view of a number of people, but the conditions that gave rise to that person in the first place, still exist and other brothers and sisters are still coming out in need of this kind of psychological change.

Urban Street Crime—Hustling

by Dr. Benjamin Carmichael

In the San Francisco-Oakland Bay Area, the determinants of criminal status among youth has changed from gang affiliation to street crimes and the related pursuit of cash money. Local communities daily bear the brunt of these crimes, as measured by spiraling crime rates.

When successful, these young criminals project a glamorous life-style which serves as a prototype for both other criminals and conventional youths to imitate. For these youths, peer status is measured in terms of one's willingness, and ability, to use deceit, cunning, daring and coercion to commit essentially petty and non-violent crimes for profit. A twenty-one year old male explained the change in youth crime as follows:

> Well, anyway, that how we (once) got our prestige; by being the toughest gang. Cutting, fighting the hardest and getting the drunkest and staying out the latest and driving the fastest cars. But now, everybody on a pimp thing. Everybody wants to have something to do with pimps. Just like a long time ago everybody would want to get some kind of job. But right now, they all want to pimp or do something against the law to get the money.

THE STREET HUSTLER

Generally speaking, the term "hustler" conjures up images of persons who manipulate other people's impression of reality; one who skillfully appraises and adjusts odds on events of chance, or who provides scarce or illicit goods and services to paying customers. In this sense, hustlers are "con-men."[1]

In present usage, however, the term hustler is applied to a category of small-time urban "street hoods" who make money through a variety of criminal means—pimps and prostitutes, small stake gamblers, fences and runners of stolen goods, thieves, burglars, robbers, small time purveyors of drugs and occasional goons. They refer to themselves as "street hustlers" and "players" and their crimes as "hustles," "games" and "ripoffs."

Street hustlers are both male and female (although predominantly male), are of different racial and ethnic group backgrounds, and typically are young (15 to 30 years old), uneducated beyond high school (although college dropouts are increasingly undertaking that lifestyle) and unskilled in anything conventional.

A few street hustlers are addicted to drugs and hustle, in part, to support their habit. Some admitted to having arrest records, dishonorable military discharges and unfavorable employment records which might be presumed to preclude their gainful employment. However, the young street hustlers I observed were distinct from most other more conventional urban youth today primarily because of their orientation to petty crime; they are convinced, and act on the assumpution, that they are skillful enough to make money, through criminal means, on a daily and ongoing basis. They believe that the odds of getting arrested can be neutralized often enough to make their crimes profitable as a career.[2]

THE HUSTLING ETHIC

The fundamental concern of street hustling is making large sums of money quickly. In turn, this money is reinvested for profit or illicit favors within a protracted sub rosa economic criminal network based on the illegal activities of local and migrant criminal, professional and organized criminals and conventional citizens and pre-criminal youth who spend money buying criminal goods and services. This network is maintained by virtue of its sheer size and numbers and a prevailing ethic of social and economic exploitation.[3]

The hustling ethic incorporates three major tenets: (1) a "situational ethic" of exploiting others, including one's personal acquaintances; (2) an extreme contempt of work, particularly manual labor and low-paying jobs, and; (3) for most non-white hustlers an obsessive compulsion to become wealthy and acquire visible evidence of wealth, such as expensive automobiles, fashionable clothes, lavishly furnished apartments and expensive jewelry.

The actual success of the hustling ethic is best reflected in the physical appearance of the hustler, particularly in his dress, jewelry and mode of transit. Successful hustlers dress to impress other hustlers and impressionable youths and drive stately automobiles with small customized "gangster windows" in the rear. Successful white hustlers, on the other hand, tend to play down their success by adopting a lifestyle suggestive of abject poverty as measured by their dress and living accommodations. Many white hustlers who are successful professed not even to own an automobile.

When evaluated over a period of more than a few years, a few hustlers can be said to have mastered their crimes or to have minimized the risk of arrest sufficiently to be considered successful. Most street hustlers who remain criminally active beyond five or six years, or after they are thirty years old, are either considerably successful or they have become what criminologist Paul Tappin identifies as common adult "amateur criminals"; those criminals who engage in general crimes requiring little organization, imagination, skill or intelligence.

RACE AND STREET HUSTLING

The variable of race among street hustlers is associated with the selection of criminal hustles, clientele to be served and the style in which crimes are carried out.

In general, white hustlers esteem drug peddling, street begging, burglary and selling stolen or "ripped off" goods. The major drugs sold are heroin, cocaine, marijuana and psychedelic drugs of all types of origins. Many street hustlers, regardless of race, will sell marijuana because of customer demand. Parenthetically, the successful selling of cocaine requires a rather steady and affluent clientele who can afford to purchase the expensive powder frequently or in great quantity because of the fleeting euphoric and analgesic effects it produces.

White street hustlers recognize pimping and prostitution as lacking character, offenses that are more associated in practice with black street hustlers. To be sure, some white females do turn tricks by hitch-hiking customers or by soliciting them on the streets. More often than not, however, the solicitation is covert and the woman's "old man" maintains a low profile. For all practical purposes, then, the white prostitute serves as both pimp and solicitor.

The crimes of black street hustlers are of four general types and differ markedly from those of their white counterparts. The offenses are listed as follows in order of their criminal esteem: (1) procurement-solicitation (pimping-prostitution), (2) gambling (cards, dice and pool), (3) purveying (selling drugs and stolen merchandise), and (4) general misdemeanors and felonies (burglary, robbery, theft, "short-con" hustles, etc.).[4] This ranking is associated with criminal income, coolness,[5] planning and risk of arrest.

PIMPING AND PROSTITUTION

As mentioned above, most street hustlers are generalists in crime: They cannot afford to concentrate their efforts on a particular offense.

The successful pimp is a decided exception to the rule of street hustler as a generalist in crime. The pimp is the most flamboyant type of street hustler and serves as the success prototype for most black hustlers.[6] The pimp's command over his prostitutes partly accounts for the great appeal, but pimping is a preferred street crime also because it tends to be financially rewarding, is associated with masculine attractiveness and is relatively insulated from arrest and retaliatory violence. After "giving game" to his women about soliciting customers and establishing rapport with and among them, little else is required of a pimp, except providing protection and occasional companionship. Clearly, the pimp epitomizes the "hustling ethic."

Woman are attracted to prostitution as a hustle, either because of a desire for money or because of attraction and devotion to a pimp. However, prostitutes often tire of a pimp and no longer wish to share money with him or no longer respect him. These women may leave and travel from city to city working as independent hustlers and prostitutes. They also may approach an already established and respected pimp and agree to work for him in an attempt to share the pimp's criminal stature.

Considerable amounts of money and criminal status may be realized by a pimp and a prostitute should they execute their hustle well. "It's a togetherness thing," remarked one pimp about this association, "It's suppose to be. Security. Me and her for her and I. Security."[7]

Prostitutes acquire criminal status commensurate with their ability to make money for their pimps. To increase their cash intake, they often devise several criminal strategies other than sex-for-pay. Often working in small teams of two or three, prostitutes rob and steal from unsuspecting customers. Some also are skilled shoplifters or "boosting broads."

THE HUSTLER IN THE CRIMINAL JUSTICE SYSTEM

Because the typical hustler is a generalist rather than a specialist in crime, he runs a greater risk of detection and arrest and is vulnerable to the caprices of a variety of individuals (including clients and other street hustlers) with whom he inevitably becomes involved. In short, if a street hustler is to be successful in crime, he must consistently "outwit the Law" and also be "several jumps ahead of his clientele."[8]

A pervasive aspect of the hustling ethic is distrust of others' motives. Distrust is exacerbated by the omnipresent prospect of arrest. Accordingly, street hustlers usually work alone or in small groups of two or three. Even so, a distrust of others' motives persists.

Since they work alone or in small groups, a hustler's absence from the street after arrest or commitment to jail may go unnoticed by other criminals. In effect, arrested street hustlers are at the mercy of the justice system. Many cope with the situation by pleading to reduced charges, thereby allowing willing police departments to clear their records of many unsolved petty street crimes; other hustlers make a deal by offering information on criminal accomplices or about unknown activities, particularly burglary and drug offenses. However, most hustlers simply "ride with" the criminal charges against them and eventually are released after serving a short or truncated jail sentence for a reduced criminal charge or conviction. The burglar in the following quotation explained this process in response to the question, "What were you charged with?" He responded:

> Five counts of burglary. Well, they tried to get me with burglary but it wasn't at night time, so they put a daylight burglary on me. That consists of almost shoplifting, but they tried to boost it up to burglary. It's a hard sentence, see. Any burglary is hard. I didn't have a lawyer. I had a public defender. If I would have had a lawyer, I would have beaten the case. But I wasn't going to put out a whole lot of money for what the judge (finally) broke down to a petty theft, which was nothing. Got 150 days, got 100 suspended, plus didn't do but 35 days, which is nothing.

Most street hustlers are insolvent and unable to meet bail when arrested. However, when arrested, a prostitute calls her pimp or bail bondsman or a "prostitute attorney," the latter retained on an *ad hoc* basis by a few successful pimps. The attorney and bondsman promise, and the pimp desires, only to get the prostitute additional time on the street so that she can make more money. Meanwhile, through legal meneuvers or because of crowded court calendars, the trial may be delayed for as much as six to ten months. During this time the same prostitute may be arrested several more times for soliciting. When brought to trial eventually, she will plead guilty to the original offense and not guilty to the remaining ones. Often, the judge drops the charges of the latter offenses and sentences the prostitute on the basis of her single guilty plea. Usually, the prostitute is out of jail and back on the street turning tricks for her pimp within a month.

CAUSES OF STREET HUSTLING

The phenomenon of hustling is not new, although the present discussion suggests that the ubiquity of the crimes, as well as the ages of those involved, may signal the rise of a unique urban crime problem; one that the justice system, as yet, is not fully prepared to address.

I would suggest that the success of street hustling is not merely a reflection of the failure of the justice system to understand and control the phenomenon. Rather, hustling survives and is supported by what may be referred to as "the criminal in all of us." Society's seeming lack of moral accountability—its situation amorality—serves to support, abet and tolerate this network of street hustlers. Members of conventional society seek out and buy the illicit goods and services provided by these career deviants.

Economic deprivation and social alienation are not sufficient causal explantations for most street hustling crimes. We know that most poor people and those who are alienated do not pursue crime on an ongoing basis as do street hustlers. Rather, the particular expression of youthful hustling that I have identified and discussed today would appear to have emerged from the pervasive social, economic and political turmoil of the late sixties. In 1967, a Presidential Commission on Law Enforcement and Administration of Justice cited the following reasons, among others, for the disturbing rise in non-violent or "ripoff" crimes:

The continued crowding together of people in impersonal urban areas;

An expanded youth population unable to find gainful employment;

The sheer abundance of things to steal and ways to do it;

The affluence that makes people less protective of their possessions;

The high cost of adequate security in homes;

A lingering tolerance and romanticizing of non-violent criminal behavior.

I suggest that these factors are still relevant to understanding the rapid rise of street hustling as an urban youth phenomenon.

STEMMING THE TIDE OF STREET HUSTLING

The criminal justice system is composed of various agencies with different priorities. The police detect criminals and make arrests; prosecutors and defense attorneys argue legal principles and the precedents of a crime; courts are arbiters and correctional officials are interested in "rehabilitation," or returning offenders back into the community. Collectively, the goals of these agencies are to cut crime and render justice. It will necessarily involve the combined efforts of all of the agencies to effectively address the problem of street hustling.

Petty crimes tend to flourish in communities in which a constant battle between police and the community exists. In order to be successful in combatting street crime, local police must establish enduring community relations. This is facilitated by heightened community visibility when not pursuing criminals and through involvement in legitimate efforts of community-based organizations. These efforts would assist police in establishing contacts necessary to gathering information about neighborhood hustling crimes. When appropriate, foot patrolmen should be assigned to areas in which hustlers are known to reside and in which they commit crimes. Foot patrolmen could better educate residents about crime prevention; how to protect homes against burglary, reject stolen goods, identify drug dealers and show outrage for local pimps and prostitutes who flaunt their activities.

Prosecutors and the courts must increase their efforts to keep proven criminals off the streets. Given their limited resources, they must still somehow accrue good, solid evidence against criminals, stress better handling of witnesses and focus on "career" criminals who repeat their crimes. Still, judges must continue to grant probation to convicted offenders for whom, in a judge's opinion, prison will do more harm than good and to persons who deserve another chance.

Rehabilitation must remain a major goal of justice administration despite recent criticism that rehabilitation programs are ineffective.[9] Informed judgements must be made about assignment to community-based correctional facilities or to state and federal prisons. The seriousness of the offense, prior criminal record and family history are important considerations in making these judgements. Concomitantly, stricter standards must be applied toward returning probationers back to jail when they are arrested on additional charges of crime. In many jurisdictions, probation is not revoked until the accused has been convicted. This is a problem area for residents of communities who are concerned about the high number of convicts on probation—or parole—who commit new crimes.

One way to decrease the likelihood that an offender will return to crime after incarceration in a prison is to ease his transition to community life. Parole—a period of supervision—or a furlough of work release serves this purpose by allowing convicts to build up a skill or a bank account while still in prison so they won't have to hustle when they get out.

And yet, as always, the most effective and direct threat to street hustling —and crime generally—is the spirit and fiber of the community itself; its willingness to work with and within the justice system; its expression of outrage and contempt for neighborhood criminals and their crimes; and its insistence that justice administration be swift, exact and fair. When these principles are achieved, we can start hustling the hustler off our streets.

REACTION

Carmichael: I think that in understanding street crime, you're talking about a different philosophical premise as far as the criminals themselves are concerned. I think that a conscious decision is made by many street hustlers to undertake a lifestyle of crime. There is a sub-cultural value that emphasizes using criminal means to make money. In the past, in order to acquire social status, one joined gangs. Many youth make a conscious decision to undertake criminal activity as a means to social status.

That means that in order to attack the problem, we must go at the source, that ethical source, that value system, that tends to give rise to criminal activity. Whenever we discuss crime, we can't discuss it in one dimensional perspective.

First of all, we need consistent law enforcement in those communities along with social programs. Community workers have to get involved in changing some of the moral principles that tend to survive in our communities. Strict law enforcement in the absence of a change of values or moral principles is going to be futile.

Cindy Sulton: It seems to me that we're all involved in a hustle, whether it is legitimate or illegitimate is the question. The substitution of a moral set of principles means the ascription to our legitimate hustle as opposed to the illegitimate hustle. But there have to be provisions for them with some benefits to be gained from it. The access is not there for the legitimate hustle. So I don't think it's a question of changing morality. I think it's a question of changing the opportunity structure.

Carmichael: I'm suggesting that understanding crime is an example of opportunity structure itself. Indeed we all hustle, but what seems to make us somehow different, many of us different, is that we still subscribe, to legitimate careers. For others this is daily orientation to crime, largely to the exclusion of more legitimate procedures.

Sullivan: I have problems with your use of the word subculture.

Carmichael: I mean the hustling ethic tends to bind together a number of people who undertake criminal means to make money. "Sub-cultural" as I'm using it now doesn't apply to the traditional notion of the term. When I use sub-cultural here, I mean a network of criminals, but not sub-cultural as related to the gang definition.

Sullivan: That network of the criminals is cultural, not sub-cultural.

Diane Palm: Let's focus on community relations, we've got to understand that we have few neighbor to neighbor relationships. There's so much fear in the black community. There's so much fear that exists there, that people don't realize that their next door neighbor has the same kinds of concerns that they have. They're even afraid to go knock on their door and tell them they've been burglarized and ask if they heard anybody or saw anything suspicious.

It's impossible for you to even begin any kind of education until folks begin talking to each other, you can forget community education, you can forget community relations, you can even forget changing hustlers cause that's not going to happen.

Davenport: If we're trying to deal with the problem of street crime, do we start by isolating those individuals who commit crimes?

Palm: I think that when we put so much emphasis on isolating those folks, we forget about all the folk who are not into this kind of life. We forget the majority of black folk do not commit crime, and we forget too that we have to begin to link up those folk to think alike, who then could possibly be a force against those other persons. I don't like the emphasis on isolation as a starting point.

Falaka: With regard to the spirit of unity; I would like to share an experience with you. Mayor Rizzo in Philadelphia requested 15,000 troops to come in last weekend. He suggested that there would be violence coming from the black community where there was a demonstration taking place as a response to the July 4th bicentennial. And there were many members of the black community who were very vocal and because of fear that the troops would come, there were negotiations between the demonstrators and those people who expressed those fears. People in the community decided that because Rizzo had said he needed fifteen thousand troops, they would prove that he did not. The word was passed in the street among people whose normal occupations may have been pimping, or burglary, and if you will check the statistics, you will find out that there was less crime last weekend than any other time this year. Black folks on all levels were concentrating on making sure that there were no incidents which could have been used as an argument for the need of troops. The street gangs passed the word to protect the demonstrators, even though they were white, Indian or what-have-you, to protect them. The commentators in Philadelphia are making jokes about the Frank scare now.
It has already been repeated by the fact that there's only six gang deaths this year whereas over the past ten years, there were forty to fifty a year. Through the development of a kinship community there was a conscious effort, to stop the killing, based on an ethic that black people are more humane than they have been displaying.

Dunning: Dr. Carmichael you didn't suggest in your paper that the Superfly Syndrome is something that we find in our communities, the part of the image. You did not suggest that violence is a necessary component of urban street crime. We find in New York it is a necessary component and one that is definitely a part of this street crime problem.
We also find that we, as a result of our studies, the hustling and the hustler, they go outside of the need or out of the area of needs, and if you will, go merely to the areas of desires, addressing those desires that fit that particular ostentation that you mentioned.

Lamb: You've mentioned several times the "systematic isolation" of certain groups, and I don't see a correlation between that and what Sister Fattah has indicated. Perhaps it's because I don't understand what you mean by isolation or systematic isolation. I'd appreciate a definition on that.

Davenport: One of the problems that I perceive in terms of crime is romanticizing the person who commits crime as a kind of a hero. Now without going through all the reasons why that system exists or the extent to which a capitalist system needs people to oppress or those kinds of questions, I'm looking at what the results are. The first thing we have to do is deal with that image of the hero, and recognizing the impact that crime has on our community from day-to-day.

The problem is to begin to distinguish those for whom the environment created or nurtured or pushed them into a negative direction from those who, as a normal kind of a practice, would engage in any sort of conduct. There must be isolation not as imprisonment but as an organizational technique.

Sullivan: There's only a small group of persons who are involved in this hero worship, if you will. Otherwise we wouldn't be here. I don't think that we have romanticized criminal activity or thought that burglary or persons who robbed someone is a hero by any means. Again we're talking about images. For us to say that burglary is good or that if you rob someone that you're okay with us again, concerns a self-image; something that we need to deal with.

But not through isolation, if you say this person's bad and this person's good, you're doing exactly what the power structure has done for years in terms of separation. We are all in this thing together. It does not mean that because you participate in some kind of activity that I necessarily have to label you and thereby exacerbate your condition so that you respond as someone different from other persons without understanding what has happened.

We must be concerned about images: about raising the people's consciousness to a level where the majority feel equipped to demand better housing. But if we begin to separate ourselves based on a standard that some other group of people set without looking at the total picture, then we are aiding the power structure in its mission. The consequence will be that we will never have any more than what we have now—economically, politically, etc.

Swan: I see the problem too as one of decisions in relationship to images. During the riots a lot of folks took things that they could not afford otherwise—a re-distribution of wealth. They were exercising their power to re-distribute the wealth in the American society. I think they're talking about something in addition to images. Really it's a question of decisions. These people are not innately bad, they just make those decisions based on opportunity or lack of it. But we have defined those decisions. It's no different from Nixon, increasing his salary while in the White House from a hundred thousand to two hundred thousand.

Sullivan: For example, the decision was made by the black community to prove that Frank Rizzo was wrong—that guards were not the answer. The black people decided to show Rizzo a community that has some organization and one that is concerned about its people.

Mr. Fattah: The street hustler is dealing on an individual level. He is by himself, on his own, needing to be creative every day; waking up trying to figure out a better way to do what he's been doing. I think we should find some ways to re-direct that energy and determination towards the whole community. Not just the United States even— channel that motivation towards solving the problems of other people in the world. There are certain people that just can't cope with collective society; they are individualistic, and I believe that these people are the ones that are the best at being hustlers and perhaps settling unconquered frontiers, given the proper training.

Kerr: In Baltimore, we are doing just that—re-directing talents and energies that young people might have into more constructive outputs. Also kids or youth get into hustling activities for the status involved. Now we have to get the community involved and turn that around so that there's no longer an accomplishment for being involved in criminal activities. In order for him to remain a leader or to have status in a community, he will have to come over to the other side and start participating in positive activities and, therefore, try to achieve status in that particular context.

Davenport: If you look at the various components of our criminal justice system, the police, the social workers, the courts and what-have-you, there has been a tendency, I think, historically for the police to have and enjoy a certain antipathy within the black community because they were thought of in hostile terms. Now to look at them differently, look at issues differently. Can we begin or are we at the point where we can say well, the police are a resource; those police who want to bring about a fairer administration of justice. I tell my law students if you want to give an impact on the criminal justice system, don't become a public defender, become a prosecutor, because the prosecutor decides who gets prosecuted.

If he decides that he's not going to prosecute you, that's the end of the case. A public defender merely responds to the exercise of power. The prosecutor has power.

Do you think that we're getting to the point that we can begin to understand that a black prosecutor is not an oppressor, but a defender?

Swan: What you just said highlights what I'm saying. Even the prosecutor has political pressures that come to bear on his decisions to prosecute. I'm saying to look at just the prosecutor is limited. And you cannot simply say don't be a public defender; the problem is much broader.

Cooper: My concern is that it appears to me that we're all so deeply involved in the criminal justice system at the local level, at the street level, that we're missing a tremendous opportunity. Across the nation, almost every state is calling for a criminal code revision. It's a priority. I don't see much black involvement in code revision across the nation.

Sister Fattah: I want to go back to the statement that was made about whether or not we were all in this together. I think we are, and I think that an example of that would be if you saw a man with his foot on someone's neck, the man can't move and neither can the person down on the ground with the foot on his neck. I think that's the situation that we're in. I don't think that anybody is born bad. We may not be able to figure out what happened and when it happened, but I know that babies don't come here as perpetrators of street crime. Okay? So that has to be dealt with in terms of the whole process, somewhere along the line.

I think also that we cannot take apart and dissect what we want to deal with. I think we have to deal with the whole thing, whether you're talking about a system that oppresses us, which it does, imperialistic crime, economics, consumer problems, street crime, it's all inter-connected, you can't just say black on black crime, it's too large for that. And I think that we would be doing a disservice to ourselves if we just took one little part of the puzzle because it isn't, it's all interrelated.

REFERENCES

1. Defined as criminals who gain the confidence of those they wish to exploit. *See* David Maurer, "The Big-Con Games," in *Observations of Deviance,* Jack D. Douglas, ed. (New York: Random House, 1970), pp. 237-51.

2. Benjamin G. Carmichael, "Youth Crime in Urban Communities: A Descriptive Analysis of Street Hustlers and Their Crimes," *Crime and Delinquency,* April, 1975, p. 144.

3. Ibid, p. 141.

4. Above discussion about appeal of drug peddling among black street hustlers taken from article, "Youth Crime in Urban Communities," *op. cit. supra.* note 2, p. 142.

5. Above discussion about esteem of black hustling crimes taken from article, "Youth in Crime in Urban Communities," Carmichael, *op. cit. supra,* note p. 142.

6. Carmichael, *op. cit. supra,* note 2, p. 141.

7. *See also* Christina and Richard Milner, *Black Prayers: The Secret World of Black Pimps,* (New York: Bantam, 1972).

8. Michael Lewis, in "Structural Deviance and Normative Conformity: The 'Hustle' and the Gang," in *Crime in the City,* Daniel Glaser, ed. (New York: Harper and Row, 1970), p. 179.

9. Carmichael, *op. cit. supra,* note w, p. 146.

Luncheon Speaker

Dr. James Q. Wilson

Thank you Mr. Woodson, ladies and gentlemen. It's an honor for me to be here, and I regard it as a most auspicious occasion because of the fact that the Urban League with its enormous prestige, I hope some day its enormous resources, has become involved in a matter of concern to everyone in the United States, and I think with the leadership of the League working through its local branches and taking the opportunity presented to us by its access to the media, can contribute importantly to reinvolving citizens in the problems of crime.

I'd like to speak very briefly and then if you wish, entertain comments or questions before this session of the program ends. And in speaking briefly, I plan to address four or five broad themes about which I am concerned which I think relate to the theme of this conference.

The first theme I would like to suggest that we all bear in mind is the enormous importance of finding a common ground on which to stand, or all Americans can stand, in the problems of crime and the war against crime. All of you are aware the criminal justice system in many parts of the country functions badly. All of you are aware that in some parts of the country it functions to the disadvantage of those it ought to help. Many of you, I'm sure, are aware of various forms of racism that have characterized that system in the past, and still continue to characterize parts of it today.

I think this phenomenon, however, has to be understood in a broader context, because although there are examples of racism, pure and simple, and they need to be identified and rooted out where they exist, there is an even more fundamental problem of which in many cases, racism appears to be the surface expression. That is that. The criminal justice system neglects systematically, in most jurisdictions, the needs and concerns of the victim. Of all the persons involved in the criminal justice system, in terms of numbers, that group which is most disadvantaged by it is the victim of crime. He is kept, or she is kept waiting in courtrooms to testify, kept waiting for his or her property to be returned, kept waiting for protection that is promised, but never delivered, not informed as to the workings of the criminal justice system, and in many cases, as a result of contact with it comes away embittered and alienated and is led to suppose that he is or she is being singled out for special neglectful treatment. Sometimes that is indeed the case, but often it is not the case that anyone is singled out, but rather than the criminal justice system functions like all other large institutions primarily to serve the needs of those who are involved in practicing criminal justice. The needs of the police are to manage their workload, the needs of the prosecutor to manage his workload, the need of a judge to manage his workload, the need of the corrections commissioner to manage his unmanageable workload, and the system functions in a cumbersome manner, but in a way, directed at those internally generated needs. And one of the functions of a national citizens group, it seems to me, is to reassert the victim's perspective on crime, to reassert the need that that system is there to serve other persons, to protect the vast majority of law abiding citizens and to do this at the local level where such expressions of concern will have the greatest impact.

This leads to the second theme I'd like to mention, the importance of community involvement in criminal justice. Now the phrase community involvement in criminal justice will strike most of you, I suspect, as a tired cliche. Who could be opposed to community involvement in criminal justice? It's a kind of motherhood issue. Yet it is one of those cliches that is a cliche only because of its repetition and not because of its familiarity in practice.

At one time, in this country, and in every country, law enforcement and criminal justice were almost entirely the function of the local community, the neighborhood, the family. It is only really since the twentieth century, that we have handed over to institutions, often run by quite competent individuals, the task of doing things that citizens once did for themselves.

In the eighteenth and nineteenth centuries, policing was done not by police officers, as we would know them today, but by nightwatchmen, typically unpaid citizens, drafted for the responsibility, who set up the human cry in the night if they found people breaking the law or menacing the public health or safety, and in response to the hue and cry, citizens came out of their homes and were obliged, expected, to participate in identifying an offender, hunting him down, dealing with the public problem, settling the dispute or the like.

As the police departments began to emerge in the middle of the nineteenth century, they emerged not because crime was on the increase, they emerged because riots were on the increase. My forefathers, Irish-Americans, who did not want to be drafted into the United States Army to fight in the Civil War, took out their feelings in a typically blunt and expressive way, by rioting in Boston, New York, and many other communities and it quickly became evident that a group of unpaid, unarmed night watchmen were inadequte to the task of dealing with this problem and hence, the move to professionalize the police and ultimately, the move in the 1880's and 1890's to arm them.

At the same time that this was happening, the police, were being told to enforce laws that for the first time, cut against the community grain, to enforce, for example, the liquor laws. In the past, the police were thought to be servants of well-established, well-understood community norms, the need to maintain order and peace, to protect property, to guard against menaces arising from a threat to public health. With passage of the liquor laws in the 1880's, 1890's, culminating with national prohibition, the police for the first time, were given responsibilities which many segments of the community did not wish them to have, and hence began a long period of conflict between elements of policing on the one hand, and the citizenry on the other, which has continued down to the present.

It seems to me that without attempting to change the entire legal context of law enforcement in the United States, it is important to attempt to redefine the citizens' relation to law enforcement and to recapture for citizen initiatives important responsibilities in this area. You know, as well as anyone, that in many communities across the United States, this is being done today. We know of neighborhood security patrols, or public house patrols, that are often organized spontaneously by community groups, sometimes with, sometimes without the active support of law enforcement agencies.

We have heard of isolated instances of neighborhood dispute settlement programs in which chronic disputes between landlords and tenants, between neighbors, among children, between gangs, are subjected to the decision, the mediation efforts and the arbitration efforts, if necessary of neighborhood groups and councils, sometimes organized along church or religious lines, other times organized along territorial lines, rather than have all of these disputes continue to clog up the criminal justice system, where the cost is not simply the monetary cost attending to these matters, but the fact that we are turning over to institutions ill-suited to handle human communal conflicts the problems of managing these conflicts. Not all these conflicts of course, can be settled at all. Some can not even be settled satisfactorily to even one party, but if there is a prospect for their settlement, if the security and good order of the neighborhood can be maintained at all, if the conflicts that break out between landlords and tenants or among neighbors or among juveniles, can be managed with any degree of satisfaction, that management will occur at the neighborhood and community level by citizens asserting their right and obligation to play a positive and constructive role in this program.

We also know that the community is going to become much more important than it has been in the past, in reintegrating the convicted offender back into the neighborhood. The studies with which I am familiar which paint on the whole, a rather discouraging picture of our ability to rehabilitate convicted offenders, nonetheless, do indicate the greater the prospects for reintegration into the community, the greater the prospects for returning to family and neighborhood, the greater the prospects for acquiring a job that is meaningful on release, and the greater the prospects for success.

And these prospects can now always be improved, certainly they cannot simply be improved by the management of distant institutional initiatives, or bureaucratic programs designed to handle this problem. These problems can only be handled when the local community is an active participant in them.

And finally it seems to me, citizen groups have an important responsibility in monitoring the functioning of the criminal justice system. Many people are dissatisfied with its functioning, not least the members of it themselves, but to find out what is happening is extraordinarily difficult. Prosecutors and judges and correctional officers are not engaged primarily in producing statistics or information. They are engaged in managing difficult caseloads in the face of extremely scarce resources.

If the community is to have a realistic idea of what in fact is happening, the community must take some responsibility in watching what in fact happens by attending trials, by visiting prosecutors, by getting involved in seeing what is in fact happening in correctional institutions. To come back with a sense of reality that does not depend, if you will pardon me, on the reports of the press. The press misrepresents this part of the system, because like all other aspects of our institutional life, it is concerned with its own needs and its needs are to report the day's news. But today's news reported in an ad hoc and sporadic fashion, cannot convey, except in the rare instance, the way in which the system, as a whole operates, and to understand that is extraordinarily important.

The third theme I want to dwell on, and a theme which I'm sure many of you know as much as I is that we must face facts that institutional programs, under the best of auspices, are not likely ever to succeed in making a significant difference in the rehabilitation of convicted offenders when these programs are applied in doses of six to twelve months, to twenty-two year old recidivists and done so in an institutional setting which militates against the prospect of success.

I don't believe that we can allow problems to grow up in our midst and to work their way slowly through the criminal justice system, have those problems solved by instructing the correctional administrator or a probation officer or a parole officer, or a special community program, to deal with this problem, given six months and a few thousand dollars per person. I don't believe it can be done when the person involved, the offender, has already spent two decades on the street, living by his wits, learning that in today's society a street hustle is often more rewarding than its alternatives. If we are going to persist in believing that these kinds of programs offer meaningful alternatives to crime, then I think we are deceiving ourselves. This is not to say that a rehabilitative, no treatment program ever works. Some programs work for some individuals, under certain circumstances.

A recent review by the Vera Institute of certain programs in New York State suggests that if you identify carefully the kind of offender and if you put them into a program that is run by dedicated individuals, it can make a difference. Certain kinds of juveniles, for example, seem to do very well as a consequence of being involved in Outward Bound programs. And other kinds of juveniles do very poorly in those programs, but do better in others.

The point however, is not that nothing works, but that our capacity to have a general solution to the problem of criminal recidivism, that can be made available to tens of thousands of persons is quite limited. Indeed so limited that we have to begin, I think, with the far broader and somewhat more challenging perspective on the problems of combatting crime. We have to take a much broader view of the generating milieu of delinquency and later of young adult and adult crime.

When I say a broader view, I do not mean what some people pose as the only realistic alternatives to rehabilitation; to lock everybody up indefinitely or spend money on combatting poverty and ignorance and disease. There are of course, important reasons why programs designed to improve the living conditions in our cities are imperative, but the argument in favor of them is not primarily a crime reduction argument. It is an argument having to do with the moral worth of eliminating poverty, eliminating ignorance, eliminating discrimination, in a society where values are directly antithetical to those social conditions.

There is a place for punishment, and apprehension and deterrence in a criminal justice system, but it's quite clear that the numbers of persons involved does not make possible, having a general policy of locking everybody up from the first offense on or keeping large numbers of offenders for large periods of time. Even if it could be shown that such policies would have a dramatic reduction on crime rates, the resources simply are not there to do it on a large-scale basis.

Well what is left, what is in between these extreme alternatives to what has been the present course of action? I think we should identify the areas in which juvenile delinquency and youthful crime begin to display themselves, and ask ourselves, have we designed institutions that appropriately recognize the stresses society now places on young people growing up, especially in the large cities.

Take for example, the family. All the evidence with which I'm familiar suggests that abusive or uncaring or unloving families are one of the chief causes of entry into a delinquent career. This is not the same thing as saying that families on welfare produce criminals. In fact the data on that are very clear. Studies I have done, studies the Vera Institute has done, show that whether or not a family is on welfare makes little difference in the production of delinquents in crime.

Nor is it necessarily the case that a broken family, a family with one absent parent, produces necessarily delinquents. There are families in which the single parent can produce as much care and support and love and discipline as is necessary. But we do have, in this society, large numbers of families, white as well as black, where neglect or abuse or uncaring attitudes are dominant.

We also have children whose control seems to elude even the best intentioned of families.

Now for the middle classes, the solutions to that problem has always been evident. The middle classes have always used certain specialized institutions to cope with that problem. And those specialized institutions were the following: They either moved to the suburbs, where the support that the street life supplies for the criminally inclined young people is absent, and the data show that persons raised in more affluent neighborhoods, other things being equal, have a better chance of avoiding a life of crime than the persons who are not.

Or they send their children to private schools or military academies or other places where, for money, the children are raised by institutions, instead of by their parents. Not in a punitive setting necessarily, but raised in an institutional setting in which the control, the regularity of discipline, the support and the nutrition, the attention to medical problems can exist, in ways which, for a variety of reasons, it might not exist in the family. These alternatives are not open to poor people, for lack of money.

It seems to me our society has been remarkably ingenious in trying to devise programs to handle delinquents after they've been adjudicated, and after they've been through the crime justice system four or five times, by which time it is almost surely too late to do much.

Similarly with schools, we have in the last several decades, in this country, steadily increased the minimum age at which people are supposed to leave school. At one time it was twelve, then it was fourteen, then sixteen, and in some jurisdictions, people talk about the need to keep people in school until they're eighteen.

As a professional educator, I'm all in favor of school. But I have to say that these institutionalized forms of prolonging adolescence are in and of themselves, contributing to the problems of delinquency.

Many children have no business in schools at such an advanced age as sixteen or seventeen or eighteen. Many would do far better if they were involved in apprenticeship programs or on-the-job training programs, equipping them for work, and acquiring skills which are best acquired on the work setting and not in the school setting. Many are kept in school under circumstances in which it is quite clear to all concerned that the only good children in school are those presumably going on to college and everybody else is on some other track, cannot contribute to the self-esteem of young persons, and young persons being naturally devilish anyway, and anxious to test authority, whenever they find it weak, delight in finding ways to subvert the intention of the schools who prolong adolescence unduly.

A study by D. S. Elliot and his colleagues in California, shows that if the study and the technique is adequate to support this, that persons who drop out of school are less likely to engage in delinquent acts than persons who remain in school if you control for, hold constant, the economic position of the family.

And the inference from that is that if, at least in California, and I don't think California is so different from other places, persons, children from poor families who are not headed for college or who for any other reason, wish to become adult, wish to grow up faster than society will allow, do better by dropping out. The problem is if you drop out now, you regard it as a dropout. And you're called dropout, the label is stamped on your T-shirt and you have to kind of wear it around all the time. You're regarded as a truant or a runaway or a person in need of supervision, a person somehow who has failed. I'm not sure that in all cases it's the young person that's failed. I'm sure in many cases it is. But in other cases, it is that we have tried to design a universal adult-producing machine called the public school system, which is not sufficiently differentiated or flexible enough to admit the fact that people reach adulthood by different routes. For many young persons, the best route to a meaningful adulthood, is not to stay in a classroom until they're seventeen or eighteen. It's to get into the labor market, or to find themselves in other ways, and to engage in activities which are more consistent with their own immediate concerns; make money, get married, have a family, be your own person and the like.

Finally, we have to worry, it seems to me, about the problem of neighborhoods. It seems to me no one can doubt that other things being equal, persons who lack all material advantages, are going to have more incentive to commit crime than persons that have those material advantages. Yet we also know that many poor people grow up without committing crime at all. In fact, the vast majority do. And we cannot assume that merely improving economic conditions will reduce crime, which is not an argument against improving those conditions, as I said before, the argument for doing that is essentially a moral one, having little to do with its crime reduction potential.

But there is one thing, however, that is clear, that if persons are living in large ghettos, be they black or white, as long as they are large enclaves of poor or otherwise disadvantaged persons, the crime rate in those areas and for those persons is going to be higher than if the same persons were living in different surroundings. A study that was recently completed compared the delinquency rates of young persons whose family background and whose income was the same, but who in the one instance, were living in a large inner-city massive ghetto, and the other instance, were living in smaller ghettos or living in different kinds of communities, and there was a dramatic difference.

There is a powerful argument, independent of the moral need for insuring that people have free access to housing, to breaking up large concentrations of disadvantaged persons. There is a powerful argument for believing that the mere fact of size, the mere existence of the South Bronx, the mere existence of the Woodward Avenue area in Detroit, constitutes a kind of reinforcement for crime that works greatly to the disadvantage of those living there, both the victims and the suspects alike.

The last point I want to make, is that we have to approach the problem of developing a new and more constructive attack on crime with a somewhat different set of attitudes than we have approached in the past. In the past, we have used the phrase, the war on crime. I wish we wouldn't always wage war when we have a problem. The war on poverty. Some people offered to surrender in that war and their offers were not accepted. Creating a war on something means we create an army of social workers or poverty fighters or crime fighters and pretty soon the maintenance of that army turns out to be more important than winning the war.

I think we have to assume that we don't really know very much about how to conduct a war on crime or how to eliminate it. And that we have to have a mood toward this problem that is compounded in equal parts with a sense of justice and a compassion and of experimentalism. We have to be concerned that people are treated fairly, and that the victimization of citizens in our cities is taken seriously. We also have to have some compassion for both those caught up in the system as suspects and those caught up in the system as victims. But above all, we have to have an experimental attitude. We have to say we've got to find out what works, we have to be willing to take chances, we have to try new strategies, and we have to be willing to let somebody else, not the people running the program, evaluate the results.

The opinion of an independent observer, measuring the knowledge they bring into the place, and measuring the knowledge they bring out of the place, as a result of my administration might come to a somewhat different conclusion. I suggest if that's true for education, it is all the more true for the criminal justice system, community involvement and the like. There have been some important major experiments in parts of the criminal justice system. People in Kansas City have tried to find out what difference it makes having uniformed patolmen driving around in marked cars waiting for something to happen. The answer seems to be it doesn't make much difference at all. People have tried to find out in California whether sending juveniles into differing kinds of rehabilitation programs will make a difference, and in the California study at least, it turned out that not much happened. People have tried to find out the relationship between involvement in the neighborhood youth corps, for example, on the one hand, and crime on the other hand.

There are some efforts to adopt this experimental attitude, to admit our ignorance, to put aside ideology and slogans, to say we're not going to approach this as a war on crime, we're not going to accuse everybody of being bad persons, we're not going to assume that crime exists because of the moral defects of those managing our institutions, or the moral defects of the members of society. We're going to assume, that crime exists for reasons that God only knows, and probably put it here, He or She, for an important reason, to test us in some way, and if He or She has been testing us, we have not been succeeding very well in overcoming those problems. We have to be satisfied, it seems to me, with modest gains and sober expectations. We're not going to see dramatic reductions in crime, except perhaps ten years from now when the baby bust that began in the 1960's is upon us, and when there are so few young people around and so many elderly people around. Either we'll have elderly people stealing handbags from young persons because social security programs are inadequate, or we won't have any crime. Of course, American society will die out in ten years because there aren't any children, but that's the price you pay for a war on crime.

If we have reasonable and modest expectations, if we assume that we have to begin very early in the life cycle of young persons, that we have to deal significantly with family, school policy, neighborhood patterns of settlement, and neighborhood involvements in the criminal justice system, we will not only have a more realistic struggle with crime, we will also, cease the terrible assumption that we can put all these burdens on the criminal justice institutions and then feel entitled to complain that they're not doing the job properly.

Thank you.

QUESTION AND ANSWER PERIOD

Lee Brown: I read your book on *Thinking About Crime* and became angered. Essentially, succinctly and very sophisticatedly I heard you saying in the book that blacks do contribute disproportionately to crime. To some extent, you dismissed as you've done today, the relationship between the social economic problems and crime and developed a program in your book to deal with greater institutionalization of those who commit crime. If my interpretation is right, the end result would be more black folks in institutions.

Wilson: I'll be happy to respond to that. The purpose in writing that book was two or three-fold. First, to try to persuade people that the Marxists are not right, that there is not a simple one-to-one short term relationship between prevailing economic conditions, on the one hand, and the level of social order on the other hand.

That crime against property went down when we had the depression of the thirties. It went up when we had the war-fed prosperity of the sixties. This is not to say, and I believe I was careful not to say, that other things being equal and in the long run, persons who enjoy middle income or higher status, will produce less crime.

But I did not want people to continue to believe, that in a generation perhaps, programs designed to raise incomes or to raise educational levels would at the same time reduce crime.

I think I also said that I'm in favor of programs to raise incomes and increase educational levels. I'm in favor of them even if they increase crime. I'm in favor of them for reasons having nothing to do with crime. Indeed, if we wish to maintain public support for programs that have these melioristic objectives, then it's important that we take seriously crime so that people will not use the increase in crime as an excuse for shutting down programs designed to alleviate real social problems.

The second point I wanted to make in that book was this: For decades, criminologists and other well-intentioned people have refused to take seriously punishment as a component, a necessary component of the criminal justice system. Not the only one, and not the sovereign remedy to deal with or solve the crime problem, and certainly, I do not agree with those who believe that if we just throw the key away that our problems will equally go away. But that punishment has to be taken seriously.

I was much hardened by the aftermath of the Watergate experience. People who had committed burglaries in order to steal things from the files of Daniel Ellsberg's psychiatrist were being sent to jail. If they'd had the sense to steal five hundred dollars from that office, or ten vials of morphine, they would not have gone to jail in California. They went to jail because they went there in violation of the public trust. It seemed to me that was a good idea; my only idea was some of them didn't go to jail longer.

When we think about white collar crime, and when we think about violations of civil rights and civil liberties, we become very angry when people responsible for those things are not punished.

I think that's a healthy attitude. It suggests that society has certain principles it attaches great support to. When people steal social security checks or rip off stores or take cars or hit people over the head when the other people are strangers and did nothing to incur it, I also think they ought to be punished. I don't know, what does punishment mean? Well it means reasonably swift and sure detection, reasonably swift and fair adjudication, and if convicted, reasonably swift and certain deprivation of liberty, or fine or monetary fine, proportional to the offense.

I think there's nothing wrong with defending that point of view. I was appalled that criminologists, not all criminologists, surely, had dismissed this as an unimportant or backward looking aspect of an approach to crime.

And the third reason I had for writing is to suggest, and here I feel very unsure of my evidence, but to suggest that there's a very close relationship between economic conditions on the one hand, and crime and criminal sanctions on the other. That they're inextricably linked. If you have a program to reduce youthful unemployment, but in other ways, you make street hustles extremely attractive, don't be surprised if people don't enroll in youthful unemployment programs.

If on the other hand, you crack down on crime, but don't have any alternatives to it in forms of reasonable jobs available for young persons, don't be surprised if the crackdown on crime doesn't reduce crime. And I think the two are very closely related. Not because people are motivated entirely by economic factors, but because there is a relationship between the advantages of alternative ways of spending your time, especially for a young person. And I think we've allowed those relationships to get out of whack by allowing teenage unemployment beginning in the early 1960's to rise to unacceptably high levels and by allowing the cost that one would have to pay for committing a crime to sink to unacceptably low levels.

Now I don't regard that as a conclusion or an attitude that you ought to be angered by, but I would be the first to admit that it's possible, I said it in ways that would anger.

Brown: Angered only in that you're in a position to influence public policy. If other people interpret what you've written the same as I have, then the result is going to be detrimental to black folks.

Wilson: Well, I don't think anybody, I don't find anybody interpreting my views, I don't find any policymakers interpreting my views in ways that would lead, I think, to the consequences you fear. But I'm sure that some might, and I apologize.

Brown: I'm sure of that, because I think what's happening now is that there's a growing belief about not only swiftness or certainty of punishment as well as mandatory sentencing, as if that's gonna solve a problem in our country.

Wilson: I don't think it will.

Brown: I know, but I'm just saying that that's a strong possibility.

Wilson: Well, at the time I wrote my book, the concept of mandatory minimums wasn't much in the air. I didn't even use the phrase, as I recall, and to the best of my knowledge, I haven't used it in my writing since. But you're quite right that inference is often drawn. It's a short-sighted inference. It seems to me the view that mandatory minimum sentences for the offenses we most fear and that are most common are not gonna make a difference except to add to the workload of the system and force the system to find new subtle ways to cope with this problem. I can think of certain offenses for which there should be. I think Charles Manson ought to face a rap that has a mandatory minimum sentence, whatever that is. But that's the unusual bizarre eccentric crime. That's not ordinary street crime for which I think some degree of flexibility is required.

Swan: Dr. Wilson, one of the things that shocks me about your book and also it seems to be a kind of Harvard mentality, is that especially the last part with respect to the correlation, and I'm assuming that you know that correlation does not necessarily mean causation, that it looks under-nourished there with little data to support the correlation.

Wilson: Which correlation?

Swan: The last one about the relationship between youth and crime and two other variables, unemployment or something. That's more your thinking, that's your opinion, that's your analysis, and that's the thing that bothers me about your work and the work of your friend Dr. Moynihan, and the work of many like Jensen. All of you seem to think that your opinion or the data must be taken seriously.

Wilson: I don't think that at all.

Swan: Well that's one of the reasons why you said you wrote your book so people can take it seriously, you said that yourself.

Wilson: Well, I think that there were some data, the data are not conclusive, but at certain points I tried to indicate why I think the data are not conclusive. And other points, I tried to indicate why I think the data are very strong. Don't use catch-all phrases like the Harvard mentality. I'm not a Harvard man. And I get a chip on my shoulder when somebody puts me there. And I don't study IQ and I don't study the economy and I don't study the things that are studied or written about by the other persons you mentioned.

I think, in descending order of significance, the data will support the following proposition, that is the strongest proposition that I think can be supported of the kind of data that I'm talking about, is that there is strong correlation among three variables, the probability of a criminal justice sanction, the teenage unemployment rate and the rate at which certain common forms of poverty crimes are committed. Now, that's a correlation, and a lot of people including myself, are working very hard to find out to what extent that is a causal relationship and one can, logically, distinguish causes from correlated relationships. I think the results of this analysis will suggest that yes, there are some causal patterns there.

How much of the crime change do these causal patterns explain? Some amount. Not a lot, ten percent, fifteen percent, something of that order.

Then there's a set of propositions about the causes of crime, or what is the generating milieu of crime? Here the evidence is very weak. Every time you think of one good argument or example a counter-example comes to mind. And then finally, weakest of all, are assertions that any given criminal justice policy, will have an effect on the crime rate or any given criminal rehabilitation program or any given crime prevention program will have an impact. Here the evidence is very weak indeed.

I am most concerned with trying to find out what works in those areas where the evidence is now weak, but I think that it is feasible and it is responsible to publish views which state one's influences, from the best available data and the relationship between crime deterrents and certain aspects of the unemployment situation. There are now at least two dozen studies done by very sophisticated people, most of them not at Harvard, with one exception, none of them at Harvard, which tend to come to the same conclusion. Whether that's going to prove to be gospel or not is premature.

There are other areas that I've talked about today where the evidence is very very weak, and I try to indicate my guarded attitude toward it.

Lamb: This conference is not only to address ourselves to the need of greater involvement or the enabling of blacks and other minorities of having some impact on the criminal justice system. We are also concerned with the need to bring about a restructuring of the criminal justice system, particularly in those areas where there is the lack of appropriate administration of justice toward people who happen to be black or other minorities. There's some research that Dr. Brown did some time ago indicating that if you are black in the United States, you are more likely to be arrested than a white person. Once you have been arrested, you are more likely to be indicted and convicted and if you are convicted as a black person, you are more likely to receive a more severe sentence than a white person. As we look at this correlation that perhaps you touched on, I get the feeling also that you dismissed in your statement the racial implications, the negative racial implications surrounding the criminal justice system. You can direct some attention to the inequities in the criminal justice system that we're all so concerned about. Just to lock up a number of black folks is something that we're very concerned about, that's a lack of equal justice.

Wilson: I understand the force of your point about insuring fairness and equal justice. It's absolutely imperative, there's no question about it.

If an absolutely fair system, an absolutely equal system had greater arrest rates or greater incarceration rates for populations that had any particular characteristic, that fact would not disturb me.

If they were also Irish or black or whatever, I would say so long as the system was fair, then the characteristics of those who are produced by that fair system are not, do not constitute a major criticism of it.

Now, then, the crucial question is under what circumstances are the fragmentary reports on the fairness of the police. I've done some in which I've found certain police departments over-arresting blacks in proportion to whites, holding offense constant, and I've found other departments in which they seemed, holding offense constant, to arrest more or less at the same rate. With respect to the prospects of conviction, in a state such as California, if you hold constant the prior record or the nature of the offense, blacks are not more likely to be convicted than whites. Indeed, for reasons I do not understand, they are less likely to be. I think I understand one possible reason that does not support the general pattern. That's also the conclusion of the study Waldo and Gerichos made of conviction rates in three states, and it is also the conclusion of the George Cole study of the California Superior Court.

On the other hand, studies done by Marvin Wolfgang and Tony Amsterdam and others point out the much greater vulnerability of blacks to the death penalty, specifically, but not exclusively in the South, and including Philadelphia, the city in which Wolfgang and Amsterdam did much of their work.

So the results are complex, but there's enough to worry you, there's enough grounds for concern such that the fairness of the system has to rank very high, indeed if there was any single criterion, I would have for any criminal justice system, any bureaucratic system, equity and fairness would be the first one, because the cost to society and to important values of having an inequitable system is, greater than the cost to society of having simply an inefficient one. Now I give this long answer because my view of the problem is that it is a complicated one, and that one's coming to grip with it, is not facilitated by adopting one of either of the two extreme, and in my view, unwarranted statements. One position is the system is fine, it's always fair, the only problem is the Supreme Court forces the system to let too many people go. But there are no other problems with it. I think that's wrong.

It's also wrong, in my view, to say that the system is thoroughly racist from top to bottom, you know, always over-arrest, over-indict, over-convict and over-punish blacks or some other minority. I believe that is also wrong. And I have not seen any evidence to persuade me that either one of those statements, extreme statements, should be taken seriously except insofar as people believe them, and of course, if you believe them, then it is a very serious matter indeed. I think the situation is complex and what one has to do is, as I said earlier in my badly prepared remarks, one has to monitor the criminal justice system with sufficient care and sufficient energy so that when one identifies unfairness or inequity, it can be immediately pointed out and people immediately brought to task.

Chaka Fattah: Yeah, I've been to most of the institutions in Philadelphia, you don't really need a study.

Wilson: I'll grant you that about Philadelphia.

Chaka Fattah: You know, to see that black people are in those jails.

Wilson: But what do you infer from that fact? The mere fact that there are more blacks in jail than others?

Chaka Fattah: I infer from it that when people speak of justice, it seems to be just us, and that scares me. I understand the problem is complex and I know the whole situation is complex, but it needs to be observed and investigated, because we are a minority of citizens but we're almost a majority in the jails. I don't think black people are born criminals.

Wilson: I don't think so either.

Chaka Fattah: That disturbs me and it should disturb someone in your position.

Dunning: I observed this morning in the workshop and I'll take you at heart when you said that was a very poor speech. Clearly, I think you missed some very important points that are the very essence of what we're about here today. I think that there may some need for a re-definition of crime, and go beyond the mere indices of the uniform crime reports. I am talking about those factors such as white collar crimes—not delineated organized crime, not delineated by the intra-structure, gambling and narcotics—that are not viewed. So I think you missed the point when you come before us and you delineate crime as being street crime as opposed to a massive intra-structure of systems and processes that refer to crime or go to crime. That's my problem with your presentation. I wish you had an opportunity to change it, but you had it written so I guess you had to.

Wilson: No, I didn't have it written, but my choice of the topic was quite deliberate. If it was poor, it was not a result of incompetence, but bad intention.

I have two reasons for emphasizing street crime. One is that it's the only kind that I have studied, although I am now beginning some research on how the FBI and other agencies try to deal with certain kinds of white collar crime. The answer in brief is not very well.

I am not going to talk about something I don't know anything about.

Secondly, I think that if you asked citizens why they're fearful, what concerns them, why people flee from the city, what contributes to racial stereotyping, it is not what ITT and Lockheed and organized crime do, it is because of street crime. And it seems to me if we don't take the perspective that what the vast majority of citizens, black as well as white, assign very high priority to, if we don't take that seriously, then we're making a mistake, which is not to say that we should neglect other things.

One of the reasons, of course, we don't have measures of white collar crime and organized crime is that almost all of this political corruption, labor racketeering, is consensual. People agree to shady deals and there is not any victim to complain. The victim is all of us, but none of us notices our victimization, so we don't call up the police and ask about it.

This requires a different kind of investigatory strategy, and we don't have a very good investigating strategy in this country for dealing with it, and I think we should, and I'm trying to familiarize myself by studying the Antitrust Division and the FBI and the Federal Trade Commission; what it is that prevents these agencies from doing what I think ought to be done.

But having said all that, it seems to me it is still proper to take seriously the citizens' concern for street crime by whomever creates, and by whomever causes it, and to worry about a system which is functioning very inadequately in coping with that aspect of the situation.

Napper: I concur that street crime is a great importance to the community, black community in particular, but I think that's because we've been basically conditioned. We can see the harm that has been inflicted upon us, and the institution that really controls the education of our people does not speak to the issue of what it is doing, does not speak to the issue of what the other major corporations are doing to harm black folks and all people throughout this country. But the point that I really am a little startled on your comment is the almost admission that racism does not play a major role in the system.

Wilson: No, that wasn't what I said. What I said was that one cannot infer from the fact that blacks are disproportionately arrested or convicted that the system is racist. That fact alone is not an adequate support for that proposition. Anymore than it was adequate to support the proposition that it was anti-Catholic when my relatives were all in jail.

Brooks: I'd like to ask you something about your relatives being all in jail. If I'm not mistaken, sometime between 1960 and 1975, the entire complexion of the prison population in the United States changed dramatically from thirty percent minorities to eighty-five percent minorities. Now clearly there was a shifting of either your relatives or mine. In the 1960's street crime was not a big issue in America, and least of all in the black communities at that time, it has grown to be a big issue. To what would you attribute this, if not racism or at least some political, some sort of massive political kind of conspiracy.

Wilson: Well, I don't think it's a massive political conspiracy. There are two questions: What caused the increase in street crime, or the perception of street crime in the sixties?

Brooks: No, I asked what caused the change of complexion of the prison population between 1960 and 1975?

Wilson: I think my best guess as to the answer is that persons who have not been excluded from society, who have not had to flee the rural countryside for cities, who have had to cope with problems of housing and jobs, institutional management, have been denied the opportunity to achieve what others before them achieved though those others themselves, when poor and disadvantaged, had been over-represented in the criminal justice system. That impediment created by a black skin is a very real one. I'm under no illusion, can't tell from the way I talk or look, God knows, if my grandfather was Irish, I certainly didn't even know that in South Boston. There's no doubt in my mind that underlying social conditions have changed too, not to the fault, but certainly to the disadvantage of black persons, their prospects for being in prison because they have changed for large numbers of persons, the relative attractiveness of crime as opposed to other alternatives closed off.

What I'm saying is not that American society does not have powerfully racist strains to it and that the management of many of its practices are not motivated by racial considerations, I would not deny that for a second. I'm only saying that at any given moment in time, one could have a perfectly fair and equitable criminal justice system, and still see the disproportionate result, and my concern is to ensure the fairness of the criminal justice system. That happens to be what worried me, which is not to say that the underlying factors that have produced the unequal access to resources and opportunities are not important. Of course, they are. I believe those will change. If I didn't believe those will change, I would be much more despondent than I am now. I don't think we're going to change those underlying factors, however, by re-defining the laws or by changing the criminal justice system. I think the underlying causes of the phenomena that you observe, rightly, are very profoundly locked up in the very nature of American society, which is slowly, painfully changing, but has a very long way to go.

Juvenile Delinquency, Juvenile Justice, and Black Youth

by Dr. L. Alex Swan

JUVENILE DELINQUENCY

In the years between 1965 to 1974, most reports have indicated an increase in the incidence of juvenile delinquency. According to reports, not only is juvenile delinquency a growing problem in America, but the increasing severity of the problem is most evident in the black community. The increasing predominance of young people in the population and the growing economic problems of the nation open the doors for the recruitment of organized crime groups of youth to participate in criminal and delinquent behavior. Most basic presuppositions concerning juvenile delinquency seem to be already known and the data accumulated on the subject of juvenile delinquency are so numerous that it implies that all we need to know in order to take appropriate action is known. However, the little action, which has been ineffective, seems to overlook the heterogeneity of the problem and the intrinsic nature of delinquency in a white supremacist, capitalist system.

It is argued that black delinquency has a significance beyond the delinquency itself. Moreover, the crimes that flourish in the black community are committed by individuals in all age groups and have their roots in juvenile delinquency. Consequently, the conclusion is that the solution to juvenile delinquency will substantially reduce adult crime.

Many theories have been advanced to explain delinquency. Independent variables range from not enough parental affection, and the absence of religious training, to poverty and police repression. The lack of employment and recreational opportunities, problems in the school system which generate a high dropout rate, racist policies and practices in the administration of justice, an active recruitment by organized criminal groups, and poor home

55

conditions have all been given some attention as independent variables which explain delinquency (Dressler 1969). However, it is agreed that a large number of delinquent acts are unrecorded in the official records of police, courts and correctional institutions (Murphy, Shirley and Witmer 1946). Consequently, police never really know the exact extent of delinquency in any community. Furthermore, youth from wealthier sections who commit the same kinds of offenses are four to five times less likely to appear in some official record than youth from poorer communities (Gold 1963).

Data collected independently of official records (case histories, personal interviews, and anonymous questionnaires) have produced findings which challenge certain relationships between some of the independent variables mentioned above concerning delinquency. For example, Clark and Wenninger (1962) agree with Nye-Short (1958) and Dentler-Monroe (1961) that there is no significant difference in illegal rates of delinquency among certain social classes.

Attempts to explain juvenile delinquency have especially examined the character of the opportunity structure available. Instead of assuming that such opportunities may provide facile models for identification, they indicate that character of the reinforcement which induces a given mode of illegitimate behavior. Not all working-class aspirants may make the grade which may lead to a career in criminal activities.

Cloward and Ohlin (1961) for example, postulate that delinquent subcultures are influenced by the availability of illegitimate means. A basis for this view can be found in Durkheim (1970) who believed that it was necessary to keep the goals of a society within the bounds of possible achievement and Morton's (1938) position that the class structure provides differential access to the approved opportunities for legitimate pursuit for culturally defined goals. However, Cloward and Ohlin claim that, aside from the limited accessibility of means to commonly shared success-symbols in the culture, the same kind of limitations exist with regard to differentials in the access of the illegitimate opportunity structures. The differentials in opportunities result, in part, from access to "learning and performance structure." They contend that not all lower-class youth will be able to achieve success through illegitimate means, and that whether or not they do will depend upon local opportunities. While it is clear that the explanations of the existence of subcultures of Miller and the social disorganization school are substantially different from Cohen's and Cloward and Ohlin's, they are in substantial agreement on one basic issue. All see the delinquent subculture as a specifically lower-class phenomenon. They all emphasize that gangs, poor school and work performance and loose home ties are special attributes of the members of this lower-class and that delinquency must be explained in terms of the social conditions in which lower-class youth are placed. Middle-class delinquency, insofar as it is admitted, is seen as an entirely different phenomenon.

Certainly, subsequent research evidence and studies do not confirm the view that upward social mobility in the industrial working class is either as limited or closed as the theorists appear to indicate. If there is considerably more social mobility than the thesis of restricted opportunity indicates, then the essential problem emerges as to how delinquents and non-delinquents differ in their responses to legitimate and non-legitimate opportunity structures. This seems to be the recurrent and invariable problem in the theoretical attempts to comprehend delinquency.

Palmore and Hammond argue that if delinquency is the product of access to legitimate means, and the availability of illegitimate means assumes that each of these states is a necessary condition for the other then lack of access to legitimate and access to illegitimate means interact to produce delinquency. If conditional relations are non-causal, neither lack of access to legitimate nor the availability of illegitimate means is a cause of delinquency, and one could manipulate either without affecting the delinquency rate (Hirschi and Selvin 1967).

Bordua (1961) writes that contemporary theorists do not account that gang delinquency "can be fun." He suggests that adolescents described in their studies are essentially healthy boys in an environment which encourages seductive delinquent activities and weak controls. Bordua questions certain basic assumptions of the opportunity theory. He notes that delinquents often find themselves blocked from occupational opportunities, but he feels it is an "end product" of a long history of their progressively cutting off opportunity and destroying their own capacities.

Spergel (1964) attempted to differentiate types of delinquent sub-cultures which he maintains are developed by the degree of opportunities available to youth in lower-classs neighborhoods. He maintains that he was unable to find the "clear-cut" neighborhoods described by the sub-culture theorists. Short and others (1965) examine the differences in perceptions of legitimate and illegitimate opportunities by black and white lower-class gang and non-gang boys and middle-class boys. An interesting finding was revealed by their study. They suggest that the logic of the theory presumes that perceptions of opportunities "precede" delinquency, but since their data reflected perceptions "after the fact" they concluded,

> It seems unlikely, therefore, that the data reported in this paper reflected the boys' efforts to rationalize delinquent behavior by "blaming" the lack of opportunity.

What is important and significant is to determine the basis of the view of the delinquents toward the structure opportunities presented them. To agree with delinquents that legitimate roads leading to goal fulfillment are closed to them, as Matza (1961) puts it, is "to join the delinquent in what is for him distortion of reality."

What criminologists are now faced with are a number of rival theories of the subculture. These theories have impacted the way in which we view the problem and seek to deal with it. Each of the theories rests upon a number of assumptions about what the subculture is really like. Matza claims that lower-class background, poor school and work performance are irrelevant factors in delinquency. It is argued that the shortcoming of the differential opportunity view of delinquency is the lack of recognition of the presence of legitimate opportunity structures in the working-class environment and the failure to perceive how these structures are utilized by some and rejected by the delinquent. In this regard the issue is one of determining elicitation of choice.

An alternative to the delinquent subculture theory has been developed by Herman and Julia Schwendinger (1969) for which they say the data were collected before Cloward and Ohlin's or sometime during their studies. They examined the total community by means of adolescent lifestyles or social types. That is, there were particular styles of life which broadly characterize most of the individuals within the adolescent community.

The Schwendingers's major social types and residual typifications seem to account for nearly all the individuals in a given population whereas other studies can account for some of the members of the community.

From their research the Schwendingers shed some light on delinquent boys' attitudes toward committing offenses. Fifty-four delinquent and non-delinquent boys were asked to play roles as "objectors" or "proponents" for a delinquent action; one example was:

> I want you to act out this story: Teenagers are arguing over whether they should beat up an outsider who insulted their club. An outsider is someone outside their circle of friends. Those who are in favor of beating him up argue with the others about it. The others are finally convinced that the outsider should be beaten up by the entire group.

The results showed that the "objectors" among the non-delinquents raised moral issues, such as the harm to be done and the rights of the victim. But among the delinquents there was "little moral ambivalence." The "objectors" among the delinquents were concerned mainly with tactical issues such as the danger of being caught. From this study there seems to be a difference between the outlooks of delinquents and non-delinquents, a little evidence for Matza and Skyes's view that delinquents feel guilty about delinquent acts and have to find moral justification for them. The interesting assertion made by the Schwendingers is that delinquents may privately have moral qualms, but that publicly they are constrained to put forward their moral views, and it is this public vocabulary which they act on; and in this sense he certainly supports Matza's thesis of "mutual misunderstanding" (Hood and Sparks, 1970).

THE JUVENILE COURT SYSTEM

The juvenile court system was thought to have represented a significant improvement over the earlier handling of juvenile delinquents. After some research on the subject, it was believed that this notion should be modified and replaced by the belief that penological philosophy—upon which the juvenile court and its related structure of delinquent control organizations were based—was a progressive ideal, a significant break with the past, but that the concept was never translated into efficient action. According to Platt (1969), however, the development of the juvenile court system which resulted in the establishment of a separate court and corrections system for juveniles, grew out of socio-political interests and a penal philosophy that were not especially liberal nor radical in nature.

Since the main object of the childsaving movement was the discovery and control of juvenile deviance, it "brought attention to and thus invented new categories of youthful misbehavior which had been hitherto unappreciated." The court system intervened in the youth's life to "save" him from a bad nature and environment denying the youth freedom without due process even when no offense had been committed or when acts for which adults were not indictable were involved.

The upper middle-class women who made up the majority of the childsavers were more concerned about the threat that urbanization, industrialization and immigration posed to their values than with humanitarian concerns for the youth. Consequently, they promoted a system which incarcerated youth for long periods of time, indeterminately, allowing for the internalization of "middle-class values and lower-class skills" (Platt 1976).

In recent years, the juvenile justice system, and especially the juvenile court, has come under severe criticism. The critics have argued that the court has failed to achieve its stated goals and has oppressed and discriminated against many of the youth that come under its jurisdiction.

Ten years ago critics argued that the courts subjected youth to arbitrary decisions and capricious procedures. These arguments led to a number of reforms that attempted to check the powers of the courts to deny youth of their constitutional rights to due process of law.

Decisions rendered by the U.S. Supreme Court in *Kent* v. *United States* (1966), in re Gault (1967), and re Winship (1970) provided for "the right to prior notice of the charges being made, the right to counsel, the right to confrontation and cross-examination of witnesses and a right not to incriminate oneself." The juvenile court is also required to adhere to the principle of "proof beyond a reasonable doubt in determining guilt." These decisions have established the fact that juveniles have rights that should not be violated and that the broad discretionary power that courts have over children must be curtailed.

For the most part, juvenile court officials have resisted adhering to many of these decisions. They have simply ignored these decisions or by other subversive strategies have not enforced these principles which would change the way in which the courts behave toward juveniles. As a consequence, individuals and groups have organized their efforts to assure the protection of juveniles through the adherence to these decisions. In the process, critics have raised questions about the court's jurisdiction over status offenders. They argue that non-criminal acts that are not considered criminal if committed by an adult should not be the concern of the juvenile court simply because the individual is a juvenile. A majority of the juveniles processed through the juvenile courts today are adjudicated for such non-criminal acts as running away, truancy, waywardness, disobeying authority, and ungovernability. Critics further argue that the description of the proscribed behavior is vague, lacks clarity and specificity and allows judges to enforce subjective standards with broad discretion. Court officials define this move as an effort on the part of critics to reduce the power of the courts by reducing the number of juveniles under its jurisdiction.

Critics argue that the status offenders are more likely to spend more time imprisoned than children charged with serious crimes. Consequently, the court is not the proper mechanism for dealing with status offenders. These and other criticisms have influenced a few state legislatures to modify their juvenile codes so as to remove status offenders from the jurisdiction of the juvenile courts.

Although this recent move in several states seems to be a progressive one, it does not deal with the entire situation. We must develop a community mechanism that impacts an internal as well as the external environment of the youth of our community.

Racism in the public schools is still pervasive and has its impact on black children. There are certain contradictions in the economic and social life of America that confuse our youth and cause them to make public decisions that get the sanction of the law and courts. Racist police practices tend to enhance the involvement of black youth with the juvenile justice system. The consequences of arrest for the black youth also have far reaching effects on future employment, education, etc.

The opportunities for abuse by the court's rules and procedures must be checked. But control of primary contacts, the determination to detain and the definition of behavior that needs special attention must be of primary concern to black people.

The juvenile justice system is plagued by failures and inefficiencies and a major effort has been made in recent years to establish cohesive guidelines for police, judges, legislators, social workers, correctional institutions and other agencies for handling children in trouble.

In light of the brutalized way in which the juvenile justice system treats children, it is a contradiction for its supporters to argue its professed humanistic principles.

A sixteen-year-old boy was arrested for a curfew violation. For this status offense he was sentenced by a non-lawyer judge to a county jail. The boy was not allowed to call his parents, neither was he afforded an arraignment hearing. Five days later he was brought before the same judge who ordered that the boy's hair and beard be cut, after which he was released in the custody of his father.

The Sixth Circuit Court of Appeals held that the boy's constitutional rights to due process had been denied. Further, the court ruled that he had been subjected to cruel and unusual punishment.

The opinion of the court read:

> A boy 16 years old is not to be slighted and his rights bandied about because of his youth by a lay judge who knows nothing of the treatment to be accorded to citizens due to his lack of experience and training in the rigorous discipline of the law. There is something rather offensive to moral decency in considering the police officer telephoning the judge that he has arrested the boy, and the judge's immediate consent that the boy be forthwith locked up in jail without the right to call his father—all in violation of the law. It is difficult to define the relationship between the judge, the police officer, and the turnkey as anything else but a well-understood collusion and connivance and avoidance of the law. *Cod. v. Turley,* 506 F. 2d 1347 (1974).

Judges with legal backgrounds also make decisions concerning youth that deny them of due process. A youth was sent to a juvenile institution after being arrested by the police in Franklin, Tennessee because the judge explained that the boy had a "bad" attitude. Not only was he not allowed to call his parents, but when his mother inquired as to where he was sent the officials would not tell her.

In many instances across the country, juveniles, simply because they are children, are not afforded full due process of law, and status offenders are not accorded the due process guaranteed applicable to children accused of criminal conduct. The fact is that presently juveniles are subject to imprisonment whether they are tried for delinquent behavior or for status offenses. Status offenders are over-represented in state institutions. The juvenile justice system is not capable or worthy of its status of "parens patriae" because the theory of its foundation is not observed in practice and it makes a mockery of such humanitarian principles.

Black people cannot afford to depend on others and the juvenile justice system to devise programs to deal with situations that impact the lives of their children in their community. Rather, black people must devise programs to deal with situations defined by black people that would impact the lives of their children in their community.

THEORETICAL CONCERNS AND PREVENTION EFFORTS

More solutions have been offered for juvenile delinquency problems than for most social problems. The techniques of intervention fall into two broad categories: prevention of juvenile delinquency and rehabilitation of the delinquent. Traditionally, juvenile institutions have been little more than reform schools where emphasis has been placed on work and discipline with little attention paid to discovering and modifying the basis of the delinquent's deviant behavior. A failure to prevent juvenile delinquency working with traditional approaches resulted, therefore, in a national concern for new approaches which would attempt to deal with particular environmental conditions that are believed to contribute to delinquency.

The logic underlying prevention, by and large, aimed to overcome factors in the immediate environment of children that seemed to contribute to their delinquency. Activities included attempts at community organization, the work of recreational and character-building agencies of all types; and attempts to reduce the commercial activities of adults which were clearly illegal and detrimental to the welfare of children who may get caught up in such traffic as, for example, the sale of liquor to minors, dope peddling, and receiving stolen goods.

Official acceptance of the logic fostered officials to conclude that improvement in the collective welfare, particularly in the welfare of depressed people, will reduce delinquency. The basic assumption seemed to be whatever contributes to the welfare and assimilation of these people reduces the delinquency rate among their children, and, correspondingly, in the communities in which they live; conversely whatever impedes their progress inflates the delinquency rate in those areas. Implicit in most of the theories and programs is an attack on poverty and discrimination. The relationship between delinquency and improvement in the general welfare, however, is more complicated than it appears at first glance. For example, although it is tempting to claim that improved housing and the reduction of poverty will reduce both crime and delinquency, evidence that delinquency is highest during periods of extreme prosperity and not during depressions, as well as awareness of the variety and number of offenses committed by middle and upper-class persons, should warn us against the facile assumption that the elimination of poverty is the solution to crime and delinquency.

PREVENTION EFFORTS

Various punitive, corrective and mechanical methods have been employed to prevent delinquency and crime. However, the corrective methods have dominated the field. Some authorities have argued that the threat of punishment and the increase of police surveillance prevent delinquency and crime. Such measures as psychotherapy, group work, casework, and counseling are employed. There also have been attempts at altering the school environment of juveniles by instituting smaller classes; expanding and diversifying the curricula; establishing special classes; and organizing remedial reading, writing and arithmetic classes. Athletic programs have also been used as a means of dissuading juvenile involvement in delinquent behavior. At another level, certain summer employment opportunity measures have been established so as to make access for juveniles to legitimate means to achieve their economic goals. Control group and neighborhood prevention groups have been organized to prevent delinquency. One of the most recent has been diversion programs which attempt to remove the juvenile from the stigma and label of delinquency so as to prevent his or her continuation in delinquent activities.

It is no secret that most delinquency prevention programs have failed. Many reasons have been given for the failure. Some critics have argued that the data collected concerning juvenile delinquent behavior have not been translated into practical terms so that a working relationship can be established between practitioners and theoreticians. Others argue that the present techniques need improving because they are presently ineffective and inadequate. It is also claimed that the nature of the prevention techniques are imprecise. As a result of these arguments, interest has been created in diversion programs and other experimental programs to control and prevent delinquency.

It could be, however, that practitioners do not have the necessary explanatory and descriptive data or the appropriate political perspective which challenge the political and socio-economic assumptions of delinquency and social control.

Becker argues in *Outsider* (1963:166) that:

> There simply are not enough studies that provide us with facts about the lives of delinquents. Although there are a great many studies of juvenile delinquency, they are more likely to be based on court records rather than on direct observation. Many studies correlate the incident of delinquency with such factors as kind of family life, or kind of personality. Very few tell us in detail what the juvenile delinquent does in his daily round of activity and what he thinks about himself, society and his activities.

It is true that since 1963 there have been some improvements in data collection. Nonetheless, the suggestion by Becker that more direct field observation of juveniles' daily round of activities, and an understanding of their thinking regarding themselves, their activities and the society is still a most valid and important suggestion.

Poveda (1970) also argues that:

> Not only must the parameters of crime and delinquency be expanded, but a new theoretical framework must be constructed which not only analyzes parts of the social system but examines the social system itself (p. 81).

As political consciousness is developed to challenge the political assumptions of delinquency and crime, and the crisis and chaos of present theoretical notions become clear, the "culture image of the criminal" will change and the prevention programs may be more realistic and effective.

What is important to understand is the nature of human action and the process development of the executed act in a capitalist-colonialist society and its creation of those conditions which produce poverty and the like.

For example, the report of the President's Commission on Law Enforcement and the Administration of Justice (1967:6) states that:

> Warring on poverty, inadequate housing and unemployment, is warring on crime. A civil rights law is a law against crime. Money for schools is money against crime. Medical, psychiatric, and family-counseling services are services against crime.

The problem of crime and delinquency is not that simple. This statement, however, highlights the need for a new paradigm. Moreover, the commission seems concerned only with apparent crime and not real crime in America.

A THEORETICAL POINT

Contrary to the notions that a reacting organism produces a sequence of action in a neuromuscular response to a set of stimuli; and that people act as they do because they have certain motives which initiate or drive the organism to action, the sociological view is that social forces cause action. One view is that human beings behave as they do because they have internalized particular norms or values which are cultural prescriptions, or rules, about behavior. The other view in sociology is that external frameworks, or structures, impose particular kinds of behavior on people. However, human beings can do much more than respond to stimuli.

Acts are constructed and reconstructed by the individual as he observes or takes note of, thinks about, and acts upon stimuli. Consequently, an act is not an outgrowth or expression of a set of causes. An act begins with the awareness of an impulse and the formulation of a goal. That is, the individual must decide what actions will satisfy his impulse and what actions are possible within the limitations of his situation. In the process of identifying the impulse and making an object of it in the form of a wish or a want, the individual plans for reaching or realizing his goal. He can control, check or even stop it. As he acts he takes into account a variety of external objects, including the behavior of other people.

Behavior need not be rational in the sense that it is wise. Many people make errors of interpretation and judgment as they plan and proceed with action. Many times they attempt to achieve goals by inappropriate methods, not always seeing the real implications and consequences of their acts. Behavior can be stupid or wise; it can involve foresight and careful analysis of preconditions and consequences, or it can be rash and irrational.

The theories of delinquent behavior do not include this perspective, thus they are inadequate especially when applied to black youth.

What can be said concerning black youth is that in the process of growing up in a hostile world—where the definition of blackness is implicit in decisions and policies to dominate and subordinate individuals and their community—it becomes difficult for the majority of black youth to make decisions that conform to the articulated norms of society. This is especially so when these norms are not practiced by those who articulate them. Contradictions are also perceived by the youth in other areas of human action and interaction.

The responsibility of the community to the youth is to provide protection from racism and oppression, and to provide services that would enhance interpetations and judgments as our youth plan and proceed with action. This responsibility is crucial in light of the fact that, for a variety of reasons, about 90% of the children who come into contact with the juvenile justice system are black and other children of powerless communities.

JUVENILE DEVELOPMENT CENTERS: BROAD GUIDELINES

Although the details of a community mechanism should be worked out by each community, broad guidelines for the establishment of such a mechanism will be discussed in this effort.

The basic principles for the operation of delivery service systems must be rooted in the broad lifesytles of the black community and the philosophical context of black people. Most agencies presently serving the community view the lifestyle of black people as deviant and in need of correction. The mechanism to be developed should have the ability to prevent the occurrence of delinquency and provide services and protection to those children who make inappropriate judgments and decisions within the context of those lifestyles.

A Juvenile Development Center should be established in each community, where there is a significant number of children and families needing protection and services. These centers, if adequately financed and properly organized and operated, can cut the number of referrals to the court, especially the truants, runaways and the so-called "unmanageables." Within the Center there should be established Family Service programs.

The processing of the juvenile must enhance the development of the juvenile's self-image and identity. When the juvenile's behavior is defined as delinquent, or where there are emotional disturbances, the community should view this as a call for aid in the form of love, support and concern.

Juvenile behavior must be allowed to be developed, nurtured, shaped and influenced by increasing the juvenile's spiritual, critical and political consciousness rather than through drugs, psychosurgery, or any other medical form of behavior modification.

The control and responsibility for processing juvenile referrals by parents who find it difficult to manage their children at home should lie solely with the Center on behalf of the parents and the community. Whatever is decided as the process of development, the entire family should be involved as far as possible. A community panel should assume the power and authority that the juvenile court judge and probation authorities presently exercise. The members of the panel should be compensated for their services.

The composition of the community panel should reflect the makeup of the community in terms of age, sex, and other important characteristics peculiar to the community. This is to assure the input from all possible perspectives in the process of development of the youth. All referrals should be directed to the respective community panel of the alleged problem. Referral agents coming in contact with the juvenile will describe the situation to the panel after a thorough investigation as opposed to labeling or categorizing the action(s). Decisions that are made by the panel in consultation with parents or guardians, should take into account the various community resources and skills in the community to enhance the process of development. What is being suggested is that the community panel act as a supervisory commission consisting of various representatives exercising community, or collective control over the administrative activities and services of the Juvenile Development Center. The commission should also provide social assistance to juveniles released from the Center whether the juveniles are in school, at work, with parents or guardians. It also should make all necessary arrangements for their work, stay in school, and their daily life— in relation to the parents or guardians whenever possible.

Voluntary community councils should be set up within the Juvenile

Development Center to aid in the development process of the juvenile. For example, there might be a community education council, community work council, community political council, community economic council, community recreation council, and a community study council.

On no occasion should the juvenile be confined to penal institutions away from the community. For those juveniles requiring services that are not in the community facilities for youth, those services should be employed to enter the Juvenile Development Center. The services of the Center should not be punitive or custodial in nature, and its management should take a humanistic approach.

Co-mingling of sexes is a natural phenomenon and should be encouraged within the context of certain basic principles so as to facilitate human development.

Each month the situation of each child should be reviewed by the panel. Whatever services are provided, the families should strengthen family ties so as to ensure that the youth continue to develop as viable members of the family and the community. Decisions to replace children in family situations should take note of these matters.

The majority of the children who find themselves before juvenile courts are black members of other oppressed communities. This is no coincidence and should not suggest that these are the only children who commit acts defined by the system's agents as delinquent. The laws which guide the actions of the agents are interpretations of the philosophy, thoughts, attitudes and values of those who make laws and those who control society. The creation of a Juvenile Development Center will provide an opportunity for the community to collectively use its philosophy and values in the process of developing its children.

The Law Enforcement Assistance Administration has recently provided $10 million for public and private agencies with innovative programs that will divert juvenile offenders from the juvenile justice system. Since it is agreed among most experts in the area that most of the episodes that juveniles engage in disappear as they grow old, it is most important that Juvenile Development Centers be established that would assist families and youth in the development of judgments, appropriate interpretations, discretions, and decisions.

Because the present services are fragmented and many duplicated from one agency to another, the services are inadequate, ineffective and insufficient. Consequently, many jurisdictions perpetuate a cycle of abuse, neglect, and delinquency in the lives of thousands of children each year. We have an opportunity to assist in the development of children and to provide the necessary assistance to families in the community that would make the difference in terms of serious acts of violence by youth. Moreover, the present practice where the neglected, dependent and abused children end up with delinquent records and become a part of the recycling phenomenon may be corrected.

The vast number of petitions presently filed each year in juvenile courts unnecessarily removing a large number of children from their homes and communities must be corrected.

REACTION

Woodson: Just one comment. I think that many families in black communities abdicated their responsibilities as parents, particularly in the sixties with the anti-poverty programs. In fact, many often looked to the institutions to provide for their own children, those necessary ingredients for life that they should have been providing.

Now, I think there's a move back toward seeing the family as a basic unit for rearing the child. All these other programs, however they're described, should be serving that particular end. Therefore, the parents will then define what services they need, how those services will be administered, and how they are to be used. That's a very important frame of mind that has to be developed. We see this concept in operation at the House of Umoja in Philadelphia. Perhaps, Sister Fattah would elaborate on this.

Fattah: I'll give you a little historical perspective on the House of Umoja, and I think you'll see the relationship between the House of Umoja and the paper so well presented by Dr. Swan. The House of Umoja developed out of the Third Black Power Conference, in Philadelphia. Over five thousand delegates from all over the country came to that conference, held at the Church of the Advocate. The main theme of the conference was survival of people of African descent, and out of the communications workshop, there were 72 communicators who decided that unless black people had some control over the media, and the way that we are presented in media, then we would never survive for another 200 years in this country.

At that time, I was a journalist and I was asked to set up the communications vehicle for the Black Power Conference. So, under that mandate, we created a magazine called *Umoja.* The magazine was distributed to universities through the black student leagues and on newsstands in Philadelphia. Coincidentally, however, in 1968 and 1969, when the publication came out, Philadelphia was experiencing 40 to 50 deaths per year. So, when the letters to the editor began to come back to my desk, people were asking questions; not so much about our role in the communications field, but very serious questions as to why blacks were killing each other, and more, particularly, why young blacks were killing each other.

So, seeking an answer to that question, and having only one person on my staff—my husband— with any real knowledge of gangs as a former gang member, we asked him to do a study into the cause of juvenile violence in Philadelphia.

The study was not conducted the way we normally study. I mean, nobody went around checking to see how many bathrooms there were, or how many TV sets. The study was conducted in the bars, in the poolrooms, in the emergency wards of hospitals. It was conducted in funeral homes and in churches, and on the street corners, and at the end of that period of time, he brought back to the group a paper which very strongly suggested that one of the major causes of the homicides was the destruction of the black family life.

There were other contributing factors, such as the influence of communications and TV. There was a certain amount of peer pressure. But, it was his feeling that the breakdown in the black family was causing the problem.

I had previously done a study on the strength of black families pertaining to us as a people thousands of years ago in Africa. So what we decided to do was to put the two papers together, because one was saying that this was the problem, while the other was saying that maybe this was the solution.

So, what we then did was to add to our own family—we have a family of six boys of our own, and we asked this group of boys to come and live with us. We promised two things to this particular group. One, we said that we would try to keep them alive, because the study showed that they were within the age group between 15 to 17, where they stood a very good chance of not being alive; and the second thing we promised was that we would try to keep them out of jail.

Out of that experience has grown the House of Umoja, which is now a group home for four categories of youth. These four categories are: One, we have a group home for boys who are dependent. I have to use the label which other folks have given us, okay. By dependent, I mean that they're supposed to be perfectly normal, except that they don't have anybody to take care of them. The second category is that they're emotionally disturbed, not psychotic, but disturbed because of family structure. These are also listed as dependent. The third category of boys are listed as delinquent. They are viewed as having had a series of contacts with the court system within the juvenile justice system. Their crimes range all the way from running away to attempted murder and rape. The fourth category of youth we have are youths who have been in institutions over a long period of time, or who have been convicted of murder, or who are now coming back out into the community, and it is felt that they need to have a period of resocialization before going back to their old communities.

We're now in our eighth year. I must say that the House of Umoja is not one house; it's 21 houses, and they're all on one block in a very small dilapidated neighborhood. Also, we've been using the same system for all four categories of our youths. Most of the youth have the same complaints. One is that there's nobody to talk to. There's nothing to do. There's an absence of opportunity and a lack of respect for them as human beings. We have provided a family for youths who don't have one, and no stake in the solutions to their problems.

There have been over 358 youths who have lived in the house, and there are only 15 of them who have re-entered prison for any violent type of activity. In terms of the program itself, we have always engaged in projects that have given the youth a lot of status. We have had gang conferences where youth, who had previously received this respect as a gang member, now get the same kind of respect by being on security duty at a gang conference.

Respect is a very important part of this. They receive recognition for committing a constructive act. We have gotten a lot of press coverage, and in some cases, they were given credit for doing something that is contributing to society. I think that is a key part of our program.

Swan: I'm just pleased by what I've heard. I wish that could go on throughout society. I think what I'm also detecting, and I wrote about it in a pamphlet called, "Notions on Suicide," is that there is a developing mode of individualism in our community, rather than a collective spirit which we once had. That, I think, speaks to the philosophy that I spoke of.

As you look at the black community, you see that we are developing a concept that "What is Mine is Mine and I'll Keep It," as opposed to "What is Mine is Mine, and I'll Share It." With this move toward individualism, there's no question about it, brothers and sisters, there's no way in the world that we are going to survive in this society as individuals.

H. Fattah: I'm also from the House of Umoja, and I think it's kind of significant that we are here today. Five years ago today, I was discharged from Camp Hill which is a juvenile state correctional institution in Pennsylvania. When I came out, I hooked up with the House, and got more involved in some of the activities around the problems affecting youth, instead of going to jail, as most black youths do after that, and learning how to become a better criminal.

When I was in Camp Hill, I had problems in terms of getting myself together because, as some of the reasons in the study stated, when you're politically aware, you threaten prison authorities; they believe you're against the system.

So, I came home wanting to do something to make sure that other youths —younger than me and around my age—wouldn't have to go through those channels of incarceration; that maybe they could be more productive in society, instead of a menace to society.

I can remember a time when a district attorney called me a menace to society. Basically, I agree with some of the things that you (Falaka) said in the study. I just wish that five years ago it was put out there.

Brooks: I'd like to back up a little bit. I don't want to take anything away from your story about the House of Umoja because I certainly support it and believe in it. But, I'm concerned about what you were saying a little while ago about the young man in San Francisco, like the one in Nashville, who was shot because the police didn't know that the house was abandoned.

I'm terribly concerned about the number of policemen, both black and white, and our commitment in America, to shooting people for things they should not be shot for. For instance, what difference does it make if the house was not abandoned? Should you be shooting someone in the back of the head who was fleeing for having removed a piece of property?

And, what are we going to do in our communities, nationwide, and with our black and other minority policemen, to get people to understand that this is only a singular response to the problem? If you're between 14 and 20, your chances of being shot in the back fleeing are much too high.

I believe that if we can bring elephants into New York City and parade them on 34th Street, and if we can get tigers out of the Serengeti without shooting them with bullets, why haven't the police in America begun to address themselves to doing something to people other than shooting them in the back?

I'd like to ask Commissioner Dunning the same question in respect to the rulings here in New York City about shooting people.

Dunning: We do have restrictive guidelines in New York as to when an officer may use his gun. An officer today may not shoot a fleeing felon; he may not shoot at a car occupied by persons unless deadly force is coming from that vehicle. As a result of implementation of that policy, we've reduced the use of firearms by police officers over 70 percent.

Now, we've had shooting because persons do not read the guidelines, or don't know the guidelines, but I can say this, that with monitoring by the public, and the fact that a police officer must report every shot he fires, we've made officers accountable and decreased the number of such incidences. If a police officer doesn't report a shooting, he's subject to department complaint and trial.

Before the guidelines, we had a comparable situation to the one that you (Brooks) gave. A few years ago in Brooklyn, police officers went into a dwelling in a black community where some youths were preparing a basement for a party. The officers entered the dwelling, ostensibly, to break up a burglary. A youth, who had been involved in the party arrangements, started to run away from the police. He was shot in the back and died. We had several days of confrontations here in New York after that with members of the black community.

Gayle: Is it true in New York City that if someone commits a crime, and is running away from the scene carrying a weapon, but not pointing it, just running away with his back turned, that a police officer can't shoot him?

Dunning: He may not shoot the gun. He'd be in violation of the guidelines unless the person running away, turned around, pointed the gun, and attempted to use deadly force.

Brooks: Commissioner Dunning, is anyone in any of the law enforcement agencies throughout the United States, considering something other than shooting people with guns?

Dunning: Yes. We're (the New York City Police Department) dealing with it. For example, we've spoken of using tranquilizers in non-violent situations, but the dosage for you may be less than the dosage for me. So, the drawback there is that a by-product of the tranquilizer may be even stronger than the use of a bullet.
We're also trying such things as a rubber-nosed projectile—it's a fist-like projectile which shoots out of a pistol. We've had some very serious results from that, not fatal, but very serious. Much is being done, but not enough to avoid the tragic situations we've discussed. Perhaps, sometime during this conference, we can take a look at the existing guidelines and edit them to fit the needs of the black community. I'd also like to suggest that we come up with possible recommendations for guidelines from this conference, and that the National Urban League be involved in developing guidelines as to when a policeman should use his gun.

Swan: Let me just say, sister (Brooks), that a police officer will shoot a black youth in a black community because he defines the youth not only as black, but also his community as powerless. He couldn't do that in a white middle-class suburb. So, it's really the acting out of that definition which allows him to do it, even if you have guidelines.

Brooks: When I talk to young people, and I ask, "Why are you carrying guns?" They say it's because the police are carrying guns. All right? My question now is that if we have done so much in the area of tranquilizers and rubber bullets, then have the law enforcement agencies in this country ever seriously considered something other than guns and gas?

Lamb: I'd like to mention the steps that Lee Brown has taken in the area of the use of deadly force in Multnomah county when he was there as a sheriff. In Multnomah County Lee established what I consider to be the most restrictive firearms policy in the country—and I have been privy to firearms policies from all around the country.

One of the things that I was most impressed with is the philosophy of Lee's firearms policy. He doesn't just relate to the legal use of deadly force and felonies, and so forth. He also speaks about the fact that the use of the weapon must also hinge upon morally and socially acceptable criteria. Perhaps, Lee, you could share your experiences with the group. I think it's important because I feel that your policy does serve as a model.

Brown: You (Lamb) essentially covered it. The policy is based on a respect for human life. The only time an officer is allowed to use lethal force is when his life, or the life of someone else, is in danger. That's the bottom line. At other times, it's not allowable.

Ward: It's a very difficult problem. Commissioner Dunning failed to mention that in New York, we don't allow warning shots anymore, and I was involved in creating this policy. It's one of the things that has helped to curtail the shooting. This is how it used to be: if a police officer shot his gun six times, he could miss a person five times, and hit him the sixth time. He could then say, "I fired five warning shots, and then shot at the person."

Well, we don't allow warning shots anymore, and it just comes right down to the fact that an officer shouldn't pull that gun to use it unless he plans to kill somebody. And, the policy also holds true for the suspect. The first time he fires his gun at an officer, that's the same as attempted murder. Now, that gets a whoop and a howl from the black community because they say that the officer didn't even fire a warning shot. Well, they never really fired warning shots anyway, those shots were just misses.

The officers often abused the whole warning shots concept. For instance, when the police and the Black Muslims had that big confrontation several years ago at the Mosque on 116th St., some of those warning shots were three feet off the ground. Warning shots! You'd have to have a bunch of midgets running around in there to get a warning from those warning shots.

The basic problem is that guns are as American as apple pie. And, there really isn't any money for gun manufacturers in making beanbag weapons and rubber projectile weapons in this country. Look at it this way: the gun a police officer uses is the same gun that organized crime uses, that a street stickup man uses, and everybody else. It's cheaper for gun-makers to make the one weapon that everybody can buy. If not, he'd be trying to arm police with a non-lethal weapon for use on the 15-year-old, and then have to produce another weapon for the guy who's an organized crime man. So, they arm them with one weapon.

The only immediate alternative is to do what Dr. Brown has done in the Oregon area, and that was done here in New York several years ago, and that is to restrict the use of guns very severely, and then back that up with tough sanctions on the police officer. We need to get state legislatures to move away from silly laws, such as shooting the fleeing felon. When this was abused in New York, the felon was usually a $100 car thief, a kid stealing for a joy ride, and then they shot him.

Peirson: I do think we need to recognize that shooting guidelines still don't supersede the law itself, so that legally, the policeman has the right to shoot a fleeing felon. In several instances, when police departments have tried to bring officers up on charges, they've been defended by the police association, or union, because they have the legal right.

So, in theory, guidelines are good, but they don't take care of the whole situation on this issue of legal force. The police have tried non-lethal weapons, particularly mace, more than anything else. Police go crazy when you give them mace, but they mace people left and right. It's non-lethal, but that doesn't mean it's not going to hurt. The use of non-lethal weapons has increased twelve times that of lethal weapons, but it still doesn't solve the problem.

Middleton: I wanted to raise a question in regard to due process of law. Don't these juveniles have a right to due process?

Swan: Yes. But, often, it's not exercised, especially in places like Tifton County, Tennessee. I'm chairman of the League of Legal Redress Committee for the NAACP, and of necessity, I have to go into meetings where these problems of our youth are discussed. Sometimes, I want to blow the place up when a judge will tell me something like: a youth had stared at a grocer with an evil look, and that he (the judge) then sent the youth off to Juvenile Hall. I'd ask the judge who had represented the youth; and the judge would say that the youth didn't need a lawyer; he needed Juvenile Hall.

Murray: That's generally true. In New York, though, youth are, in fact, represented in the Family Court, and I think the lawyers representing them on assignment do a pretty fair job. I'm biased in that regard. But, overall, there is a tremendous amount of ambivalence and resistance on the part of some very well-meaning people.

I'm involved in Legal Aid in New York City, and I've found that social workers and probation officers often complain the loudest and most frequently about a lawyer somehow doing his youthful client a bad turn because he insists that the client get all the rights that he or she is entitled to. Many of the personnel within New York City's Family Court system come out of a background that says they should operate on the theory of the child's best interest. But, they have never quite squared with the notion of the child having some basic constitutional rights. Once accused, they expect the child to lay down, roll over, and play dead. Anybody who insists that the prosecutor must prove the child's guilt, is essentially accused of not dealing in the child's best interest.

It comes out of the same notion that Dr. Swan was talking about—a kind of noblesse oblige by the middle-class white lady who wants to do something for the poor, deprived youth. But, when that youth says that it should be proven that he was the guilty party, somehow it's a different story. Now, these are very well-meaning people who just haven't adjusted to the notion of due process for juveniles.

H. Fattah: Is there any kind of law which says that a youth arrested on a charge, and proven not guilty of that charge, can still be incarcerated because the judge might feel that the youth has come before him too many times? Or, can the judge just exercise his discretion?

I want to know because that's what happened to me. That's how I went to Camp Hill. The judge said that if he let me back out on the street I might do this or that, and that I had a record for this, and a record for that, and he sentenced me to the institution.

Dunning: Yes. You might have been freed of the charge you were originally arrested for, but the judge has the discretion to use his social perspective in dealing with the total child, or maybe even the total family. For the Persons in Need of Supervision cases, you know the child, the judge might feel that a child could get better services with the assistance of a social agency, and that, at that time, the child might not get those services within his own family or outside the social justice system, for want of a better word.

Swan: Another thing that I've been pushing for with respect to that in regard to adults is that associated charges should often be dismissed. For instance, if I'm stopped for running a red light, and I explain to the policeman that I didn't run the red light, he might then arrest me for resisting arrest, or some other thing. Now, if I'm found not guilty for running the red light, then I think those associated charges should also be dismissed. I argued that before a group of council people in the State of Tennessee.

It's true, though, that juveniles are incarcerated even when they're not found guilty. The judge sometimes might say that the youth has been before the court too many times, and he'll send him back to the juvenile detention center.

   H. Fattah: Point of information. The judge who sentenced me to Camp Hill sat on the state crime commission. The commission's annual report had stated that if any youth, who came before a judge, had an alternate remedy to incarceration, that the judge would abide by the youth's wishes.

   At that time, I had an alternate remedy. I was going into the Army. But, I was a known gang leader, and even though an Army Sergeant was in court saying that as soon as the charges against me were dismissed, he was ready to take me into the service, the judge didn't pay any mind to that. He said, "I'm going to sentence him to Camp Hill anyway." His mind was closed.

SELECTED BIBLIOGRAPHY

Becker, Howard S. *Outsiders: Studies in the Sociology of Deviance.* London: The Free Press, 1963.

Bordua, David J. "A Critique of Sociological Interpretations of Gang Delinquency." *Annals of the American Academy of Political and Social Science,* November, 1961, pp. 126-136.

Clark, John P. and Eugene P. Wenninger. "Socio-Economic Class and Areas as Correlates of Illegal Behavior Among Juveniles." *American Sociological Review,* 27 (December 1962), 826-834.

Cloward, R. A. and L. E. Ohlin. *Delinquency and Opportunity.* London: Routledge and Kegan Paul, 1961.

Cohen, Albert K. *Delinquent Boys: The Culture of the Gang.* Glencoe, Ill.: The Free Press, 1955.

Dentler, Robert A. and Lawrence J. Monroe. "Early Adolescent Theft." *American Sociological Review,* 26 (October 1961), 733-743.

Dressler, David. *Sociology: The study of human interaction.* New York: Alfred A. Knopf, 1969, pp. 245-247, 431, 565-574.

Durkheim, Emile. "The Normal and the Pathological," in *The Sociology of Crime and Delinquency.* Edited by Wolfgang, Switz and Hohnston. New York: Wiley, 1970.

Gold, Martin. *Status Forces in Delinquency.* Ann Arbor: University of Michigan, Institute for Social Research, 1963.

Hirschi, Travis. *Delinquency Research: An Appraisal of Analytic Methods.* New York: The Free Press, 1967.

Hood, Roger and Richard Sparks. *Key Issues in Criminology.* London: World University Press, 1970.

Matza, David. "Review of Delinquency and Opportunity." *American Journal of Sociology,* 46 (May 1961), 631-633.

Morton, Robert K. *Social Theory and Social Structure.* Glencoe, Ill.: The Free Press, 1938.

Miller, Walter B. "Lower Class Culture as a Generating Milieu of Gang Delinquency." *Journal of Social Issues,* 14 (1958), 5-19.

Murphy, Fred J., Mary M. Shirley, and Helen L. Witmer. "The Incidence of Hidden Delinquency." *American Journal of Orthopsychiatry* (1946), pp. 686-696.

Nye, F. Ivan and James F. Short. "Reported Behavior as a Criterion of Deviant Behavior." *Social Problems,* 5 (Winter 1958), 207-213.

Palmore, Edmund B. and Phillip E. Hammond. "Interacting Factors in Juvenile Delinquency." *American Sociological Review,* 29 (1964), 848-854.

Poveda, Tony G. "The Image of the Criminal: A Critique of Crime and Delinquency Theories." *Issues in Criminology,* Vol. 5, no. 1, (Winter 1970).

President's Commission on Law Enforcement and the Administration of Justice. Washington, D.C.: United States Government Printing Office, 1967.

Platt, A. T. *The Child Savers: The Invention of Delinquency.* Chicago: University of Chicago Press, 1969.

Schwendinger, Herman and Julia. "Delinquent Stereotypes of Probable Victims." Cressey and Ward, ed., *Delinquency, Crime and Social Process.* New York: Harper & Row, 1969.

Short, James and Stodtbeck. *Group Process and Gang Delinquency.* Chicago: Chicago University Press, 1965.

Spergel, I. "An Explanatory Research in Delinquent Subcultures." *Juvenile Delinquency.* Rose Giallombardo, ed. 1964.

Bridges Over Troubled Waters:
A Perspective on Policing in the
Black Community

by Dr. Lee P. Brown

As we deliberate on the general theme of this symposium, it is important that we do so with the recognition that never before in the history of this country has the system for the administration of criminal justice been under such close scrutiny and public criticism. As America celebrates its Bicentennial, its system of criminal justice is also on trial. Many of those who find themselves disenfranchised are focusing unprecedented attention on the criminal justice system—a process they see as being riddled with inequalities. Rather than rendering her verdict without regard to race, creed or color, Justia, the Goddess of Justice, stands accused of having removed her blindfold and thereby reflecting in her decisions all of the bias inherent in a society where color is relevant.

If we accept the premise that America is a "government of laws, not men," we must also accept the fact that men make the laws and men personify the system for applying the law. It is this process for the application of the law that we call the criminal justice system. It involves police, prosecutors, courts and corrections. For most Americans this system works well—that is for most white Americans. But for others (e.g., poor, blacks, browns), the system is seen as a tool of the power structure. The apparatus for the administration of criminal justice is viewed by a substantial segment of the population as being oppressive. The inequities of the application of the law can indeed be seen by examining criminal justice statistics. Studies have revealed, for example, that in proportion to their number in the population, blacks are more likely to be arrested than whites. If arrested, they are more likely to be convicted. Prison statistics reveal that once convicted, blacks are more likely to be placed in institutions. When imprisoned, they receive longer sentences than whites.

To fully understand the magnitude of the inequities in the administration of criminal justice in America, it is necessary to explore all components of the system. Since others are covering the prosecutor, courts, and corrections, this paper will concern itself with only the first agency in the system for the administration of criminal justice — the police.

In recent years, blacks have engaged in extended (though necessary) rhetoric about the police establishment. I feel it is now time to move to a different level of concern. The rhetoric, however, has served a purpose by focusing attention on the pervasive problems of police service in the black community. It is now time to develop strategies for eradicating undesirable police practices. It is time to make some basic decisions followed up with decisive action.

If real progress is going to be made toward making the police responsive to all enclaves in the community, efforts must be extended beyond mere symbolic issues.

It is being suggested here that in order to effectively deal with undesirable police practices, one must first of all understand the police structure (both formal and informal), the social milieu in which the police must work and how the structure, social ideals and philosophies affect the individual police officers. In addition, it is important to understand how the police role is re-inforced and supported by the interest of a dominant power structure and how all these concerns relate to the policing of the black community.

The purpose of this paper, then, is to examine the police system by focusing upon the police as an occupational subculture. This approach is essential because:

> The problem is not one of a few "bad eggs" in a police department of 1,000 or 10,000 men, but rather of a police system that recruits a significant number of bigots, reinforces the bigotry through the department's value system and socialization with older officers, and then takes the worst of the officers and puts them on duty in the ghetto, where the opportunity to act out the prejudice is always available.[1]

It will be pointed out that there are certain structural and organizational defects in police agencies that prohibit the mere getting of "good men" from having a significant impact toward eradicating the inequities in the police establishment.

The paper will focus briefly upon the political structure and ideology of the community in order to place into focus a true understanding of the role of the police in respect to society. It shall be pointed out that the police are not indifferent, rather they are responsive to those in any given community that possess the power. To illustrate that the police are not responsive, in a positive way, to the black community (those who are powerless) a few examples of police abuses in the black community will be discussed.

In concluding, the paper will suggest that the solution to the problem is decentralization and some form of police accountability, as opposed to the gadgets and gimmicks that have been perpetrated upon the black people through police-community relations programs.

POLICE SYSTEMS IN AMERICA

Policing in the United States cannot be viewed as a single police system. Rather, there are over 17,500 separate law enforcement agencies employing approximately 450,000 persons and spending close to 5 billion dollars per year. Police agencies are located at three levels of government: (1) federal law enforcement agencies, (2) state police agencies, and (3) local police agencies serving counties, cities, townships, villages, boroughs and unincorporated towns. Most of the nation's police agencies are at the local level. The size of agencies vary from the New York Police Department with over 30,000 officers to several jurisdictions with only one policeman. The average police department consists of ten men. Our concern, obviously, will be with policing in the cities which have a substantial black population. This problem was adequately dramatized by James Baldwin when he wrote:

> The only way to police a ghetto is to be oppressive. None of the police commissioner's men, even with the best will in the world, have any way of understanding the lives led by the people; they swagger about in twos and threes patrolling. Their very presence is an insult and it would be, even if they spent their entire day feeding gumdrops to the children. They represent the force of the white world and that world's criminal profit and ease, to keep the black man corraled up here, in its place. The badge, the gun and the holster, and the swinging club make vivid what will happen should his rebellion become overt. . . .
>
> It is hard, on the other hand, to blame the policeman, blank, good-natured, thoughtless, and insuperably innocent for being such a perfect representative of the people he serves. He too, believes in good intentions and is astounded and offended when they are not taken for the deed. He has never, himself, done anything for which to be hated—which of us has? And yet he is facing, daily and nightly, the people who would gladly see him dead, and he knows it. There is no way for him not to know it: There are few things under heaven more unnerving than the silent, accumulating contempt and hatred of a people. He moves through Harlem, therefore, like an occupying soldier in a bitterly hostile country; which is precisely what, and where he is, and is the reason he walks in twos and threes.[2]

Using Baldwin's assessment as being descriptive of the problem, our next step is to develop an understanding of the situation and to explore remedies for correcting it. This can be accomplished by exploring the police role in the community.

POLICE AND THE COMMUNITY

Although we previously pointed out that there is no single police system in America, it might be even more appropriate to say that there exists almost as many police systems as there are police departments. This difference in policing styles can be attributed to the fact that the police tend to reflect the community setting in which they operate. Thus, there is a direct relationship between the homogeneity of the community and the polarization between the police and the community. In homogeneous communities, where there exist similar cultures, values, class, race and status, the police tend to be responsive to the controlling power structure of the community. Thus, the young, the poor, and the minority groups (the powerless) view the police as an army of occupation because the police are supportive of the status quo and represent that which is seen as the sources of their oppression. Reflecting the attitudes of power structure, it is no wonder Jerome Skolnick, in his study of the Oakland, California Police Department, found anti-black sentiments to be the norm rather than the exception among the policemen in that department.[3]

Similarly, Professor Albert Reiss, Director of the Center for Research on Social Organization at the University of Michigan, in his extensive study of the police in one city found:

> In predominantly Negro precincts, over three-fourths of the white policemen expressed prejudice or highly prejudiced attitudes toward Negroes. Only one percent of the officers expressed attitudes which could be described as sympathetic towards Negroes. Indeed, close to one-half of all police officers in the predominantly Negro high-crime rate areas showed extreme prejudice against Negroes. What do I mean by racial prejudice? I mean that they describe Negroes in terms that are not people terms. They describe them in terms of the animal Kingdom. . . .[4]

Seemingly, the anti-black attitudes are not new. To the contrary, the 1935 Harlem Riot Commission Report claimed, "The Police of Harlem show too little regard for human rights and constantly violate their fundamental rights as citizens. . . . The insecurity of the individual in Harlem against police aggression is one of the most potent cases for the existing hostility to authority. . . ."[5]

Study after study has revealed that the police have strong anti-black feelings and therefore cannot be considered neutral forces in the community. According to Lohman, the "police function is to support and enforce the dominant political, social, and economic interests of the town, and only incidentally to enforce the law."[6]

POLICE ORGANIZATION

It is significantly important in discussing the police to understand that police agencies are bureaucratic and quasi-military. Being bureaucratic, police departments are divided into a number of specialized units. Each unit has a specific responsibility: (1) *Administration*, (Chief of Police) which is concerned with the management of the department and determines the overall policies and procedures, (2) *Investigation*, which is concerned with the follow-up investigation of offenses (detectives), (3) *Juvenile*, similar to detectives, only they handle cases involving juveniles, (4) *Traffic*, enforcement of traffic regulations (writes tickets) and investigates accidents, (5) *Patrol*, the uniformed unit of the force that patrols either on foot or in radio cars and responds to calls for service or intervenes into people's lives upon their own discretion.

Being quasi-military, police departments have a chain of command characterized by a centralized command system. Even though large cities are divided into precincts, the overall policies and procedures are still determined by administrators at the central headquarters.

Not fully understanding the organizational structure of the police and its relationship to city government, many protests against them have been directed at the wrong spot. Traditionally, when a group launches a protest against the police, they direct their efforts toward the chief of police. To their surprise, nothing happens. This is because the chief of police is subordinate to and often serves as a buffer for the chief administrative officer of the city—city manager or mayor. It is the elected officials that are vulnerable to public criticism and not necessarily the chief of police.

To fully understand the police, it is important to realize that in addition to the formal police organizational structure, there is also an informal police organization. Thus, an examination of the formal organization of a police agency will probably not reveal any evidence of discrimination or double standards. The policies and procedures of the formal organization, to the contrary, clearly advocate objectivity, equal enforcement and the absence of discriminatory practices. Consequently, when one attempts to prove charges of discrimination and dual standards, it is almost impossible because the official policies and procedures can be used to disprove the charges. In the final analysis, charges against the police often boil down to the word of the policeman, and often more than one policeman, against the word of the complainant.

When we talk about the informal police organization, we are referring to the individuals that comprise the organization. We are referring to the human beings that are fitted into the boxes that are neatly drawn on an organization chart to depict the formal organization structure. We are talking about the individuals that enter police service with the minimum of twenty-one years of social exposure behind them. For that reason, we will now focus our attention on the human aspect of policing.

Discretion is an important part of police work. Unlike private business where the administrators exercise more discretion than their employees, the patrolman exercises more discretion than the chief of police. Working with the minimum of supervision, the patrolman uses his discretion to make many decisions. He decides whether to invoke the criminal process or not. It is he who decides to stop and question "suspicious" people. Thus, the decisions which he makes are apt to reflect his personal attitudes not only toward law and morality, but also the people he deals with. If we can understand this point, we can understand why studies have shown that the majority of the police are prejudiced. Since the same social machinery that produces everyone else in the society also produces the police, the police only mirror the attitudes of the society. If that society is prejudiced, can we logically expect the police to be any different?

One would think that police administrators would make provisions to change the anti-black attitudes of police officers—or at least control the negative behavior that stems from those attitudes. This assumption, however, presupposes the existence of capable and competent leadership within the police establishment. An examination of the process by which one becomes a chief of police will dispel that assumption. The common and traditional method of becoming a police chief is to be promoted up through the ranks; thereby assuring in-breeding.

Without lateral entry into the managerial positions in the police establishment, the thought of seeing positive changes occur is often only wishful thinking. The current state of police leadship, with a few notable exceptions, is in bad shape. Police departments are being run by many men who are incapable of understanding the need for change, not to mention having the ability and imagination to bring about change. To the contrary, most of them got where they are today by being conformists. Maintaining the status quo, therefore, provides them with a certain degree of security in that they believe their successful career stemmed from the fact that they did conform—so why change? According to one leading educator in police administration:

> There is ample evidence to indicate that many American police administrators are narrow-minded, parochial, tunnel-visioned individuals who are frightened at innovation and who perpetuate ineffective and archaic law enforcement. Two-thirds of our police administrators have never attended college. Less than . . . [15] percent have a college degree.[7]

Even the future for law enforcement leadership is not very encouraging if one were to examine those who are currently entering police service. Not long ago, for example, a federal commission released results of its 18-month study and reported that many police departments across the nation are staffed with poorly trained officers who never should have been recruited in the first place. Those are our future police leaders.

The informal organization of the police is so powerful that even if police departments did have competent administrators there is strong suspicion that the police would still not be responsive to the black community. This is because, as previously pointed out, the patrol officers exercise a great deal of discretion in the performance of his duties. He decides to intervene or not, to arrest or not, to mistreat or not. These decisions are influenced by the officers' attitudes toward black people.

Increasingly, white police officers are being recruited from the under-educated and politically conservative ranks of the society. Many enter the department having never even talked to a black person before. His ideas toward blacks were informed vicariously from his parents, his friends, the schools, and the predominantly white news media. He probably does not live in the city; rather in the suburbs. If he does live in the city it would probably be in an all-white, segregated section. For example, 87 percent of the Chicago police officers live in two segregated areas of the city. Thus, their daily exposure is in segregation and discrimination (housing, education and even in the case of the police department, employment). Such individuals are recruited into the police department and assigned to work in the black community. He is poorly trained to carry out that function. He brings with him attitudes that reflect his subculture, e.g., white, working class. Only stupidity would prevent one from seeing the built-in conflict which is destined to occur under these conditions. The officer is going to experience culture shock, because the black community is far from being a carbon copy of what the officer is accustomed to. In "self defense" he is going to over assert his authority and thereby perpetuate the attitude that all policemen are "racist" and "brutal."

It is also important to understand that police unions and associations constitute a source of power and they are traditionally anti-black. Illustrative of this point is the Fraternal Order of Police (FOP), representing almost 130,000 members with affiliates in over 900 different cities. During a past presidential election, John Harrington, then president of the FOP, came out publicly in support of George Wallace for President. Similarly, the politically powerful New York Patrolmen's Benevolent Association (PBA) by running a blatantly racist scare campaign, was able to defeat the referendum to create a civilian review board for the New York Police Department. The political power of the PBA can be seen in that it was successful, with help from the John Birch Society, in defeating the issue even though it had strong support from such powerful men as Mayor John Lindsay and Senators Robert Kennedy and Jacob Javits. According to Skolnick:

> Police organizations such as the Patrolman's Benevolent Association, conceived of originally as combining the function of a trade union and lobbying organization for police benefits, are becoming vehicles for the political sentiments and aspirations or the police rank and file, as well as a rallying point for organized opposition to higher police and civilian authority.[8]

Indeed, the PBA is on its way to becoming one of the most powerful lobbies in the New York State Legistlature. It, along with similar organizations see ". . . themselves as the political force by which radicalism, student demonstrations, and Black Power can be blocked."[9]

THE POLICE MISSION

The interpretation, articulation and implementation of the police mission further adds to the fuel that polarizes the police from the black community. The police, similar to many other American social institutions, had its beginning in England. The structure (and mission) of the police in America does not have its roots in the protection of the rights of the black people. Nor have black people had a voice in determining the police role. Furthermore, the police have not attempted to become a part of the black community and sincerely win its respect.

Rather, the police have developed as their role the protection of life and property. In respect to the first mission, the protection of life, this turns out in reality to be the protection of white lives and particularly the white citizens from blacks. This can be seen in the philosophy of a Southern sheriff who bragged that in his county there were three types of killings. "When a white man kills a black man, that's justifiable homicide. When a black man kills a white man, that's murder. And when a black man kills another black man, that's just another dead nigger."

Again, this disregard for the lives of black people can be seen as an extension of the regard white society in general has for blacks. Illustrative of this point is the case of a Unitarian minister, Rev. James Reeb, who went to the South a few years ago to participate in the civil rights struggle. Rev. Reeb was killed. Also killed was a young man by the name of Jimmy Lee Jackson. The death of Rev. Reeb prompted President Johnson to get on nation-wide television and give his famous "We Shall Overcome" speech. The White House sent Rev. Reeb's widow flowers. Ironically, Jimmy Lee, who died first, was not mentioned by President Johnson. Jimmy Lee's parents did not receive any flowers from the White House. Interestingly enough, Rev. Reeb was white and Jimmy Lee was black. This form of non-verbal communication reflects the attitude that to white America, the lives of blacks are meaningless. This attitude is carried over into the police forces.

The words of the Sheriff of Los Angeles County also add substance to the charge:

> We are supplying our men with more modern and more sophisticated equipment. I do not intend to publicize where this is stored, nor precisely what the equipment is, but we are better prepared from a standpoint of weaponry to contend with our problem than we have even been. . . . I have been asked if high-powered rifles, automatic weapons and tear gas projectiles are available to all Los Angeles County Sheriffs Deputies at this moment. The answer is yes. When needed, they are available at a moment's notice.[10]

Is there a question in anyone's mind as to where such weapons are to be used? The answer becomes unavoidably evident when looked at in terms of the findings of a study conducted by the Institute of Social Research at the University of Michigan which from "a representative sampling of American men found that sizable minorities want police to shoot to kill in putting down ghetto disorders and destructive student demonstrators. . . ."[11]

The role of protecting property also serves to exclude the black community from being part of the police's favorable concern. When the police patrol the white community they are in fact protecting the property of that community. For example, often when a white police officer sees a black man in an all-white neighborhood, almost without hesitation, he will stop and question the man. In doing so, he is performing his role of protecting the property of the community from outsiders, e.g., blacks. Contrast this with a situation in which a white officer sees a white man in an all black neighborhood. Again, without hesitation he will stop the man and warn him about the hazards of being in the area alone. In the former case, the police are protecting the white neighborhood from the black man; whereas in the latter, he is protecting the white man from the black neighborhood.

The property which the police do "protect" in the black community is likely to belong to a white absentee landowner. Thus the service he renders in that regard is not a service for the black community, but a service for a businessman that leaves the community each night.

In essence, the mission of the police was developed for white people and not black people. The police consider themselves as representatives of the white community and not the black community. Hence, within the black community, the police are indeed looked upon as an occupying army protecting the interests of the ruling class in a neo-colonial setting. Thus, within the black community, police harassment, police brutality, police corruption does exist. These abuses do not accidentally occur and they are not acts of malice on the part of the individuals. The abuses are built into the police system by virtue of its composition and organizational structure, and maintained by the articulation of the police mission. Void of power, the black community remains the unfortunate recipient of misuse by police authority.

RECRUITMENT AND SELECTION

A significant element of concern within the black community is the small numbers of blacks in the police departments. The absence of black faces adds credence to the charge that police departments are racist institutions. Although blacks make up about 12 percent of the nation's population, only about 4 percent of the nation's sworn police officers are black.

To understand why there is such a small number of blacks on police forces, one has only to examine the recruitment and selection process utilized by police agencies. It is at this point that inequities that are perpetuated throughout the agency begin. The recruitment and selection process is not conducive to attracting divergent personality types with different political ideologies. To the contrary, the entire process serves to screen out individuals with different cultural backgrounds and philosophical ideologies than the norm of those who are currently within the police system. That norm is being white and ultra-conservative.

The exclusion of blacks is accomplished in two ways. First, by not attempting to recruit them and second by systematically excluding those who do apply. As pointed out by the President's Crime Commission, ". . . there can be little doubt that in many communities, both in the North and South, discrimination in the selection of officers has occurred in the past and exists today."[12] Contrary to the rhetoric of many police administrators, little sincere effort has been made toward attracting blacks into police work. Washington, D.C. is a notable exception, but over three-quarters of the population in that city are black. To do otherwise would be an act of pure stupidity. There is also ample evidence to indicate that a number of departments have used an unwritten token quota for blacks on the police force. A New York City police officer put it in these words: "When I was appointed to the department there was a definite quota system. They would only appoint a certain number of Negroes. The investigating officers had their orders, and they would just knock men on petty things."[13]

TRAINING

Even if the police candidate enters the police service as a man of good will, it is in the academy, according to Niederhoffer, that the umbilical cord that binds the police to the community is severed.[14] The training given in the police academy today has little bearing on the reality of the world the rookie will face once he leaves the academy. The instruction within the academy is conducted by white individuals, often other officers, who teach from a white perspective about white laws, white sociology, white politics and human relations from a white viewpoint. Double this with sleep-inducing lectures on rules, regulations, policies and procedures of the police agency, the rookies leave the academy totally unprepared to work in a black community. The problem is further complicated by virtue of the fact that once he is assigned to a coach, the coach advises him that whatever he learned in the academy does not work on the street. That advice is correct, but for the wrong reasons. What he has learned in the academy does not work on the street because he has been conditioned to view his role as that of enforcing the law and not serving the people. Having not been prepared for what he will encounter in the black community, the recruit experiences cultural shock. He does not see white middle-class individuals such as himself. Rather, he's exposed to people of a different hue, with different mannerisms, dress and speech. He is exposed to, probably for the first time in his life, the products of a racist society. There, he comes in contact with people who have been poorly educated, who are badly housed, and who are unemployed. He is confronted with people who are angry and view his presence as being the representative of the sources of their oppression. It is for that reason that James Baldwin wrote, "Their very presence is an insult, and it would be, even if they spent their entire day feeding gumdrops to children."

DISCIPLINE

The police method of handling citizen complaints against policemen has been described as "the world's biggest washing machine. Everything that goes in dirty, comes out clean." Most large police departments have some form of internal affairs unit to investigate complaints made against officers. Even so, the most frequently heard complaint lodged against police procedures is about the manner in which they handle such complaints. Being a close-knit occupational subculture, the police are very protective of their own. Thus, as observed by one police official, the ". . . police continue to receive huge numbers of complaints but there are only a few instances where the complaints are upheld. They can't be wrong that much—and we can't be right that much."[15] Such conditions led to the conclusion by a Michigan State study team that "probably the strongest criticism that can be offered is that seldom is meaningful disciplinary action taken against officers guilty of one or more of the forms of brutality."[16]

Illustrative of the self-protective attitude of the police and how blacks continue to suffer from police abuses because police administrators refuse to deal effectively with officer misconduct is the case which occurred in Hartford, Connecticut. On November 14, 1970, a Spanish organization sponsored a dance in a predominantly Spanish section of Hartford. During the dance, a minor disturbance erupted and the police were summoned. The majority of police who arrived on the scene were white. One of the white officers arrested a young Puerto Rican woman and in doing so, with the assistance of another officer, dragged her by the hair and limbs toward the patrol wagon. A black officer observed that in addition to being injured, the girl was being subjected to public humiliation and voiced his objection to the white arresting officer. At which point, the arresting officer released the girl, turned around and struck the black officer on the side of the head. The black officer hit back and after a brief scuffle the two officers were separated. Upon returning to police headquarters, the black officer was suspended by a white captain. The white officer was not suspended. Following the suspension, the chief of police then initiated an investigation of the fight. On November 20, 1970, the Hartford Guardians released a statement that read in part:

> The time is at hand when Black and other minority police officers and citizens cannot and should not, stand by and permit white, bigoted police officers to unjustly assault and abuse the dignity of Black, Puerto Rican, or for that matter, any human being. If it becomes necessary for Black officers to physically interfere in further unjust acts of police brutality, then the public can very well look forward to a new breed of Black Officers. In good faith we cannot and shall not permit Black and Puerto Rican womanhood and manhood to be exposed to such bigoted abuse. The days of the "yas suh—no suh" officer is almost over.[17]

The Guardians felt that the investigation of the incident was not fair and impartial because the superior officers made a prejudgment in suspending the black officer and not the white officer. In addition, the investigators were friends of the white officers. As it turned out, a police department hearing was instituted and the black officer was found guilty of striking the white officer and given a twenty-day suspension. The Hartford Guardians commented on the results as follows:

> The unjust punishment of the officer . . . is not unusual because every minority race policeman experiences the "Kangaroo Court" justice he has received. Every minority race policeman is always considered guilty until he proves himself innocent.[18]

If the police department cannot convince black police officers that they, the black policemen, can receive an objective and fair investigation, how do they hope to convince the black citizen that he will be treated any differently?

The case just cited was used to point out the fact that the police are very self-protective. The police administrators are often paternalistic when it comes to handling complaints against officers. Some administrators not only overlook violations, but actually foster misconduct by not disciplining the officers who are obviously guilty.

REWARDS

The police reward system parallels the police articulation of their mission. That is, the police identify with the law enforcement aspect of their job more so than they do the service aspect. This is true even though studies have shown that the police spend only ten to fifteen percent of their time dealing in actual law enforcement activities and eighty-five to ninety percent performing some service not associated with the enforcement of the law. Because they identify with what they do the least, they are rewarded for making the "big pinch." Good police work means making arrests.

Most departments have some system for giving recognition to the officer that does a good job of police work. The more daring the arrest, e.g., shoot-outs, or the more serious the crime, the higher the reward. For example, one morning a San Francisco police officer was leaving the police station enroute to his beat at the beginning of his shift so he could get his first cup of coffee. On his way, a broadcast came over the police radio of a robbery in progress. The officer was only a block from the scene of the robbery and therefore was able to get there in a matter of seconds and effect the arrest. For this piece of "good police work," he was given the next to the highest award given by the department. Later, he was told by a superior officer that if there had been shooting involved, he would have received the highest award.

The ". . . traditional methods for measuring and rewarding of efficiency of both individual officers and organizational units place no positive value on the quality of the police response in other than crime-related situations."[19] If the officer is only rewarded for "crook catching" and given no recognition for treating people decently he simply does not have any incentive to be a public servant.

TACTICAL FORCES

Most large city police departments have established special tactical forces of officers that have no specific beat assignments like the regular patrol officers. Rather, the tactical forces can be assigned to a specific high crime rate area when needed. This practice is called selective enforcement, or saturation patrol.

The logic behind saturation patrol is understandable because there is a need for additional officers as a result of the high crime rate. The areas in which the tactical forces are assigned, however, usually turn out to be in the black community. This practice, according to one expert, ". . . replaced harassment by individual patrolmen with harassment by entire departments."[20]

Roving tactical forces are often moved into the black community without prior warning and conduct intensive street stops and searches. Obviously, a large number of innocent people are stopped and they attribute the stops to their being black. Because the tactical force is mobile, it has no ties to the community nor is it responsible to the district commander. In addition, the officers assigned to the tactical forces are predominantly white, thus adding to the resentment.

In summary, the conditions which we have just described were succinctly discussed by Levy when he wrote:

> First, the police departments recruit from a population (the working class) whose members are more likely than the average population to hold anti-Negro sentiments; second, the recruits are given a basic classroom (training by trainers who) are more likely than the average population to hold anti-Negro sentiments; third, the recruit goes out on the street as a patrolman and is more likely than not to have his anti-Negro attitudes reinforced and hardened by the older officer; fourth, in the best departments, the most able officers are soon transferred to specialized administrative duties in training, recruitment, juvenile work, etc., or are promoted after three to five years to supervisory positions; fifth, after five years the patrolman on street duty significantly increases in levels of cynicism, authoritarianism, and general hostility to the non-police world. Finally, it is highly likely that the worst of the patrolmen will wind up patrolling the ghetto, because that tends to be the least-wanted assignment.[21]

POLICE-COMMUNITY RELATIONS

A little over a decade ago, police-community relations programs were started and at that time held great promise for destroying the barriers that separate the police from the community. Obviously, this has not occurred. Police-community relations programs have not delivered what they promised.

Looking back in retrospect, police-community relations programs were destined to fail from the beginning. Most were hastily established because it was fashionable to have one. Some were created to "prevent riots." In both cases, the programs were given little, if any, direction and virtually no authority to deal with the substantive issues of the community. In many cases, the existence of the unit was contingent upon conditions that it did not do anything—don't rock the boat. In other places, the unit became a dumping ground for the officers who were misfits in other units.

Police-community relations programs were ill-defined. Even today most existing programs would be better labeled public relations programs in that they exist for the major purpose of improving the police image. For example, a major community relations endeavor of one city consisted of an expensive public campaign involving radio, television and billboards encouraging the public to "Wave at a Cop—He's Human Too." Another city's sole police-community relations program consisted of sewing the American flag on the officer's uniform. To date, most police-community relations programs are no more than gadgets and gimmicks.

The problems of the black community are too pervasive to attempt to improve the police image in the community by using public relations gimmicks.. The residents of the black community are concerned with the everyday chore of survival in a community in which the infant mortality rate is over two times that rate for the city as a whole. They are concerned about conditions that attribute to their community having a death rate twenty-five percent above the city's average. Black people have to deal with food poisoning and venereal diseases that are 100 percent higher than the average of the city. They are daily confronted with the end results of a racist society—alcoholism and drug addiction. Their community has an illiteracy rate above fifteen percent because the schools are the poorest and the equipment and books are too old and mutilated to be used in schools. Consequently, three-fourths of the people do not finish high school and mental retardation is five times that of the city as a whole. They do not have jobs because of discrimination. Consistently, twenty-five to forty percent of the black teenagers are currently unemployed. The community has to survive on an average per capita income which is only sixty percent of the average for the city as a whole. In the black community there is overcrowding, dirty streets, poor transportation and an extremely high crime rate.

These conditions are viewed, as the results of oppression perpetuated by a white power structure. White racism is seen as the source of their frustration and the white police officer that comes into the community is seen as the representative of that oppression. Couple that with abusive police practices and we see why the hostility directed toward the police is not unlike that directed toward a foreign army of occupation.

The above represents one end of the pole. The other end is characterized by the attitudes of the white community (including white police officers) and those pacification programs that have been introduced in the black community under the title of police-community relations.

Police-community relations, as traditionally defined, developed and implemented in the black community is dead. It is impossible to sell the black community on the idea that the "policeman is your friend" as long as there exists racism, discrimination and corruption within the police department. Black people cannot and will not identify with a police department which they see as over-policing and under-protecting the black community. The situation is ironic because blacks are the greatest victims of crime and suffer the most from criminal acts. Therefore, they need police protection more so than other segments of the community. Consequently, there exists a dire need for the black community to develop strategies to effectively deal with the police. The inverted power relationship in which the police have more power than the people they "serve" makes the traditional concept of police-community relations meaningless.

POLICE ACCOUNTABILITY

The black community, for the most part, looks upon police as outsiders with no ties, interest or allegiance to their community. Thus the police are seen as the "Thick Blue Line" of oppression that derives its authority and direction from an established political and economic order outside of the black community. Hence, "A major element of the police function is to maintain the value structure of the prevailing social order."[22] Thus, the police orientation is directly delated to the social, economic, political and geographical plight of black people in America. That is to say, there exists a caste system in America that places blacks in a subordinate position. The police is the authority of the dominant class within the caste system and thereby personifies its tenets, philosophy and ideologies.

It should be clear by now that in discussing the police and its relationship to the black community we are dealing with the issue of power. The police of any given community have been and shall continue to be responsive to those who possess the power in that community. If blacks cannot control or at least have a meaningful input into the power system that prevails in a community, they shall continue to be the victims of abrasive police practices. That is because on a formal basis, those who control the power influence and/or dictate to the police. They also have an inherent interest in maintaining the status quo. On an informal basis, the police identify with the prevailing power structure. Thus, psychologically, the police feel that they must defend that which they identify with, which in turn perpetuates prejudicial and authoritarian practices in the black communities. As long as the controllers of a community who also control the police are prejudiced, the police will respond accordingly.

Seemingly then, if it is the value system of a community that creates the problem, then there is a need to alter that system. To quote Frederick Douglas:

> Power conceded nothing without a demand. It never did and it never will. Find out just what people will submit to and you have found out the exact amount of injustice and wrong which will be imposed upon them; and these will continue till they have resisted either with words or blows or with both. The limits of tyrants are prescribed by the endurance of those whom they suppress.

It is inherent in the American tradition to provide the mechanism for ending suppression of oppressed people. The Declaration of Independence, for example, says:

> But when a long train of abuses and usurpations, pursuing invariably the same object, evinces a design to reduce them under absolute despotism, it is their right, it is their duty, to throw off such government, and to provide new guards for their future security.

A community that finds itself disadvantaged by the dominant value structure of a prevailing social order must change the system that is the source of their disenfranchisement.

The most obvious solution lies in a transformation of the power within the community. That would involve transforming the black community from a condition of powerlessness to a status of having social, economic and political power.

I do not foresee that occurring in the near future. Therefore, it becomes necessary to deal with the problem on a more pragmatic basis. That will entail developing a system whereby the police are in fact responsive to the people they serve. For this to occur, the inverted power relationship between the police and the black community must be changed. There is a need, in other words, for making the police accountable to all segments of the community.

In the Report of a Discussion Conference on Community Control of the Police co-sponsored by the Institute for Policy Studies and the Center for the Study of Law and Society of the University of California at Berkeley, three models for establishing community control over the police were discussed:

1. Neighborhood political control over on-the-beat policemen through elections of neighborhood commissions with full or considerable power over the police, or the creation of new neighborhood-based police.

2. Creation of counter-police organizations (in effect "unions" of those policed) with a political base and an ability to hear grievances and force change.

3. Transformation of the police profession and role so as to end isolation of the police from the rest of the community, and thus establish *de facto* community control by informal, rather than formal, means.[23]

The latter two models, for all practical purposes can be forgotten.

The creation of a "counter-police organization" has been attempted. As a matter of fact, the Black Panther Party got its start as a counter-policing organization and quickly realized the necessity to move to more meaningful endeavors. The Watts Community Action Patrol failed in its attempt to get federal funding for its activities because the Los Angeles Police Department flexed its political muscle. Let it suffice at this point to say that the black community has not been able to develop enough political power to counteract the community power structure in general, and specifically the power base of the police who identify with and influence the community power structure.

The same criticisms would apply to the probability of achieving "Transformation of the Policeman's Role and Career." The responsibility of policing and the importance of the job dictates that it not be left to a force of "non-professionals." The Black community needs the police, only it needs a police force that serves and is responsive to their community.

The answer then, seems to lie in the first-model, neighborhood control of the police.

The concept of community control of the police is not without precedents. For all practical purposes, there exists community control of the police in the suburbs and in counties. Since our police system in America had its beginning in Europe, we might look again to Europe for another precedent. As noted by the Berkeley report:

> Civilians do not just oversee, but actually run most European police departments. . . . This substantial degree of civilian control and influence in the police forces has probably assisted them in responding to present-day challenges.[24]

Before exploring the concept of community control over the police, it is first of all necessary to develop a workable definition of what is meant by community control. Keep in mind we are talking about the question of power; therefore to be meaningful, community control must consist of more than mere efforts to influence policies or to individually or collectively affect policy through pressure groups. Meaningful community control must involve more than a collective voluntary association of people who have no legitimate power. To be effective, community control must involve a model whereby the community representatives can exercise legitimate authoritative policymaking. It must involve the formal possession of power and have quasi-governmental status, as contrasted to the status of a voluntary civic or pressure group. It must be more than a group of selected individuals serving with the consent of a superior authority, because participation without power is no more than a ritual.

It should be pointed out here that it is not the intent of this paper to develop a definitive model for community control of the police; rather only to express some ideas. Hopefully these ideas will be provocative enough to lead to the development of a definitive and workable model.

In developing a model for community control of the police, we must be mindful of the need to develop one that is workable and has a chance of being implemented, otherwise we will only be indulging in an intellectual exercise in futility. Again, this involves giving careful consideration to the prevailing power structure. Not doing so, for example, was one reason for the defeat of the referendum to establish neighborhood control over the police in Berkeley, California. The prevailing power structure is not going to relinquish control of the institutions that are used to keep them in power. The Berkeley Model called for the establishment of three separate police departments, one for the black community, one for the white community and one for the university community. The department would have been separate and autonomous. By mutual agreement, they could use the same facility but each department would be administered by fulltime police commissioners. The commissioners were to have been selected by a Neighborhood Police Control Council composed of fifteen members from that community elected by those who live there. Each department would have five community council divisions within it. The councils would have the power to discipline officers for breaches of departmental policy or violation of law. They could direct their police commissioner to make changes in department-wide policy by majority vote of the five department commissioners. The Council could recall the commissioner appointed by it at any time if it found that he was no longer responsive to the community. The community would recall the council members when they were not responsive to it. Finally, all police officers would be required to live in the area covered by the department they worked in.

The major criticism of that model, which I call the "Segmented Model," is that it called for the creation of three separate and autonomous departments that never came together at any level. It would be likened to a pyramid without the apex. On a practical basis, however, the referendum did not pass because it would remove the control of the police from the prevailing power structure.

Petitions to place the Segmented Model on the ballot were circulated in cities throughout the nation as a part of the Black Panther Program. They were successful in getting the issue before the voters only in Berkeley, and in that case, it was defeated by an overwhelming margin.

A case study of the Segmented Model reveals that it is not going to be adopted (it also had great opposition from many blacks); therefore, it is necessary to develop an alternate model.

An "Aggregate Model" of community control of the police appears to be the answer to the problem. Such a model would not separate and create autonomous police departments, but would give the black community a position of parity and power in making policies relevant to the black community.

The Aggregate Model would involve decentralization of the police function and changing the police organization structure by implementing the team policing concept; thereby doing away with the militaristic structure.

In decentralizing the police function, cities would be divided into police districts, the same as or similar to existing police districts. Each district would have a Board of Police Commissioners, elected by the residents of that district. The Commissioners would serve on a part-time basis similar to the city councilmen of many cities. They would be paid for their services. By city ordinance, that Commission would be given the authority over certain police functions in the district. Essentially, the Commission would have control over personnel (e.g., training) and police policies and procedures for that district. The Commission would be essentially a policy making body. Individual members of the Commission would have to reside in the district from which they were elected and would be subject to recall.

The actual administration of the police assigned to the district would be up to a professional police administrator, chosen by and responsible to the Commission. This district police commander would carry out the policies of the Commission.

Essentially, this model would make the police accountable to the community for their action. Yet, it does not create separate police agenices. Many police departments currently have district precincts with precinct commanders. The difference would be that under the Aggregate Model, the commander of the precinct would be responsible to a local policy making body composed of citizens and not a distant centralized administrative staff. This arrangement is advocated because, as Lindsay wrote, even the most expert shoemaker is unable to know where or if the shoe he makes pinches. In other words "It is sadly instructive to find what a gap there always is between the account even the best administrations give of the effect of their regulations and the account you get from those to whom the regulations apply."[25]

By not proposing to abolish the centralized administrative staff, e.g., chief of police, this model would close that gap.

A representative from each District Board of Police Commissions will be elected or selected to serve on the Board of Directors of the citywide police agency. (It is being assumed that all segments of the city will not opt for neighborhood control because they are not dissatisfied with the police service they currently receive—thus necessitating a centralized police agency to serve those areas, e.g., white middle and upper class areas.) The chief of police would serve as chairman of the Board. A sub-committee of the City Council would also serve on the Board of Directors, thereby not removing city government from the policy making process. This Board of Directors would develop general police policies and procedures and be responsible for the staff and auxiliary services such as a central personnel department, planning and research, records and communications, housing and material, jail management and criminalistics. The representatives from the community would not only have input into those general policies and procedures but would be part of the policy making body. This Board, by a vote of no confidence, could replace the Chief of Police.

At the district level, the para-military structure of the police organization would be changed. Instead of the pyramid structure in which each man is answerable to a superior officer in the chain of command, the district policing would be done by three self-contained policing teams. Each team would be headed by a team manager and assigned an eight hour shift. Enough officers and supervisors would be assigned to each team to perform all necessary police functions on that shift. Organizationally policing at the district level would look as follows:[26]

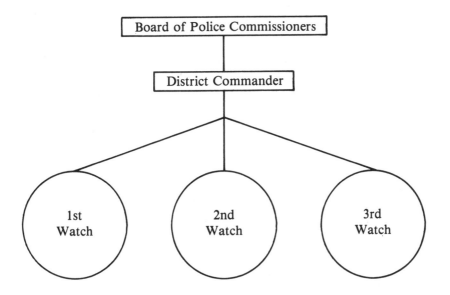

The team managers would meet periodically with the District Commander. The District Commanders, in turn would periodically meet with the Chief of Police and the central headquarters staff. Such an arrangement would assure coordination and cooperation in all matters.

There are an obvious number of details that would have to be worked out before implementing the Aggregate Model. Implementation, however, should not require any more than the passage of an ordinance and an election in the districts.

In conclusion, it goes without saying, a substantial percentage of the black community do not trust the police. The end result is a large percentage of the crime that is committed in the black community goes unreported. Equally important, this element of mistrust results in many members of the black community not giving the police that information necessary for them to successfully carry out their mission. Blacks are extremely reluctant to serve as witnesses. These conditions are deeply rooted in the history of American policing and today represent a legacy that hampers even the most honest attempts to deal with the persuasive problem of crime in the black community.

To successfully deal with the problems being addressed by this symposium, we need police leaders that are imaginative, innovative and sensitive to the unique problems of their black citizenry. With notable exceptions, that is not the case in American policing today.

We need police chiefs that consider their entire community, including the black community, and not just the prevailing power structure, in developing police policies, procedures and operations. With notable exceptions, that is not the case in American policing today.

We need police departments that have a minority representation in proportion to the minority representation in their communities. Almost without exception, that is not the case in American policing today.

We need police training programs that provide the police officer with an understanding, appreciation and respect for cultural differences based upon ethnic and racial backgrounds. Almost without exception, that is not the case in police training programs today.

Succinctly stated, we need a mechanism whereby the black community can make input into the police policy issues that affect their community. That indeed is not the case today.

Absent the above, some form of community is called for.

> . . . community control is an issue transcending education, police, or any specific urban function. It is an issue intimately involved with the demands of democratic theory and it cannot be discussed without reference to that theory. This does not prove that, in our present circumstances, democracy entails decentralization or that we can justify decentralization by referring only to democracy. It does mean that those opposed to decentralization ought to consider the meaning of its rejection.[27]

The adoption of some form of community control might very well mean the salvation of our cities. Community control is the most realistic nonviolent means of social change.

REACTION

Swan: There is a question of accountability and identification. Historically, police do not see themselves as accountable to black people or their community. Neither do they identify with them. During the 1917 riots of East St. Louis, white folks left the community and invaded another community; it's the only one in history where this happened.

Police identify with those people who they sense can legitimize them, and how do we build into our communities a system to legitimize police to the extent that they then feel accountable to us? And then in fact, identify with the community.

Brown: In my community control model, there is decentralization with some simple power to hire and fire those police officers who reside in a particular area that's decentralized.

Cooper: Have you considered the notion of possibly having a separate career ladder to deal with the large portion of work that's now being done by grossly unprepared policemen?

Brown: Yes, I have considered that in the process of developing what I call a community service officer, the whole issue involves a demilitarization of the police. There are three levels; a community service officer, a public service officer, a public safety officer and supervisors.

I see merit in having policemen involve themselves in all aspects of police work. Police are a service agency and not just a law enforcement agency.

The strategy goes beyond just the police. It's really the black community developing sort of political power; that's the strategy. My model calls for a very simple mechanism of passing a city ordinance. That's very simple. So the mechanism for doing that is political power.

Lamb: With people in positions such as yours, Reggie Eaves, Hubert Williams and others, are there efforts made to hold police officers accountable for the discretion that they use? Officers can, you know, have a whole series of options that they can take into consideration, and they take into consideration without clearly defined grounds or direction. Is there any where in the whole business of change that is taking place with blacks in present positions to bring in some accountability?

Brown: The main thing to be done with contemporary policemen would be to develop guidelines, rules or regulations that govern what a police officer can do. I think the accountability really comes from an existing system; who you would have running that police agency. The police administrator can perpetuate the abuses by not dealing effectively with them when they occur. The police are very paternalistic, there is a concern about whether or not I have the support of those, I'm talking about police administrators, whether I have the support of the men who work for me. If I come down hard on this person, what will be the union's position, what will be the other police officer's position? Will I last as a police administrator? There is the whole question of longevity that exists in the police agency. I place a lot of emphasis on the existing structure, on who you have in that position and that person's willingness to try things that are non-traditional.

Brooks: I want to go back to the whole black community thing. As much as we feel about black policemen and as much as their role has been either good, bad or indifferent, we really need them. We really need blacks on the police force in black communities around the United States. In light of the realities of the whole police system, I mean the whole law enforcement system, what appeal would you use to get good, young brilliant, humanistic black men to come into the force?

Brown: I don't think it's impossible to get young humanistic black people to come to the police force. The problem's been that historically, they have been excluded from doing so.

I think also that there is a problem in what happens when you get there. In police work, there is a strong socialization process. Because one is black, you have not necessarily escaped that socialization process. There is a strong demand on police to conform to the existing mold of the police establishment.

For example, I entered police work, the first thing I was told, the sooner you act like everyone else, the sooner you'll be accepted.

What I would suggest is that there is a necessity of doing more internal changes so that the black policemen will not have to tolerate a lot of the abuse that he does as a police officer.

Dye: Many young men are not interested in becoming coppers. On the other hand, many are intimidated by the vibes that they're going to get from their own community in terms of being police officers; it takes quite a constitution. That's a lot to ask of the young black man to come on into the police department and try to conform as much as possible into the system.

But, if we don't ask, what are we going to do for protection?

Hargrove: Well, these surveys that we've done in the National Black Police Association on examinations, have shown us that the black applicant or the minority applicant has been far and above the percentage of the white applicant. So the desire, I think, is there. It's the fact that the system keeps them out, not the desire to come in.

Brown: I know that at Howard we did a study of the black policemen in the District of Columbia called the attitude and perceptions of the black policeman through the Center of Urban Affairs and Research. Essentially what we found was that those who were currently with the D.C. Metropolitan Police Department had an interest in becoming a police officer at a young age. We also found that their reason for wanting to become a police officer was different from white folks. They were more interested in being of service to the community—that's an important variable.

Third, we found that they were very much aware of the inequities that go on amongst blacks and amongst police officers and how they treat the black community. An overwhelming majority felt that they themselves, as black officers, did not get equal treatment within the police department. I think that that's a key point.

Hargrove: Along with that political influence to impact the system, we must try to rock that boat from the inside. What's happening in most police departments in America, where they have a substantial number of black policemen is that we're upsetting their norm. We are no longer telling them that we're gonna be blue. We're telling them we're not going to stand by and witness this brutality act. We have mechanisms and laws in this country that are beautiful, that everybody ignores.

We started complaints in the National Black Police Association against LEAA, Department of Justice, they have beautiful guidelines for compliance review that they totally ignored. As a result of our agitation, they set up a minority advisory board. Yet now they have decided, arbitrarily, to eliminate the black police element from the advisory committee that started the whole ball rolling, and dangerously enough, somebody might sit down in that committee and allow them to do it. So I'm saying that we have to disrupt from the inside.

Hassan Fattah: Perhaps the black community could bring in a black security company, hire a black security company to protect their community which would take the whole thing out of the hands of the police force, you know, unless called in. Or we could train blacks to come in and patrol with the police officers. The House of Umoja started a program for training brothers from the street, in police work. There are some pilot programs that are attempting to get off the ground where people from the community will come in and patrol with the officers. But in order to do that, we have to have the political power to follow it up in terms of getting the city councils and so forth to support that. A pilot project could be set up in black neighborhoods to see if it would work.

Hubert Williams: The heart of the matter is the ability of black folks to control what happens in local police departments. The ability to control the political process. The city gets its power from the state. We elect our mayors. We are at a point in time now in this country where we have literally hundreds of black mayors throughout the country. We did not have any black people commissioners or top officials in police departments that were actually running them until we began to get some black mayors. We didn't get black mayors until black people represented a substantial portion of the city. We've noted that once we begin to reach the point where we take on a bit of power, that the rules of the game change. Now the rules are beginning to change; the unions are going beyond the cities, which are controlled by blacks, to the power base that created the cities, the state. They're exercising power and authority in the state government to control what happens in the cities that limits the ability of the people that live in the cities. So that unions can go to the State of New Jersey for example, once the Supreme Court rules that all police officers of the city have the power to make police officers live in the city, and once the Supreme Court of the United States holds that the law is constitutional, then the unions get the state to eliminate the laws, and pass a new law, to exempt police from that provision. So police officers can live wherever they will. There are several factors that we must control. We must begin to control the hiring process, the promotional process, and policies in police departments. All precipitates from political power.

In the State of New Jersey, the hiring process and promotional process are controlled by civil service. Civil service is a state institution. But we can recognize the political realities and the political reality of the situation is that you must control the political process in order to begin to impact on what's happening in police departments.

But before we can begin to gain the kind of power that will have a significant impact, we must begin to make certain that the mayors of our cities and those people that we elect in our cities are sufficiently politicized to what's happening in the police department and will expand their power to the point where they can influence what happens in the state. That's where the new game is going down, and if we don't control, if we have no influence on what happens in the state government today, I can guarantee that it won't make a damn bit of difference what the people want in the cities. They'll change it every time in the state, and the only way we can do that is to get down into raw politics; the politicians that are black, the police commissioners that are black, the police officers that are black, and that people that are black have to recognize that they got one common problem, and that's the fact that they're black. And once they begin to realize that, I think we can develop the necessary political power base to affect what happens in these police departments. If we don't do that, we're not gonna affect nothing, we're gonna be back to the age of rhetoric, and rhetoric has gotten us nowhere.

REFERENCES

1. Levy, Burton, "Cops in the Ghetto: A Problem of the Police System," *American Behavioral Scientist,* Vol. II. No. 4, (March-April, 1968), p. 31.

2. Baldwin, James, *Nobody Knows My Name* (New York: Dell, 1962), pp. 65-67.

3. Skolnick, Jerome H. *Justice Without Trial* (New York: Wiley, 1966).

4. *Report of the National Advisory Committee on Civil Disorders* (Washington, D.C.: United States Government Printing Office, 1968), p. 160.

5. Skolnick, Jerome, *The Politics of Protest* (Washington, D.C.: United States Government Printing Office, 1969), p. 184.

6. Lohman, Joseph D., "On Law Enforcement and the Police: A Commentary," (Paper Presented at the American Association for the Advancement of Science, New York, December, 1967), p. 26.

7. Germann, A.C., "The Problem of Police-Community Relations," (A Paper Prepared for the Task Force on Law and Law Enforcement, National Commission on the Causes and Prevention of Violence, October, 1968), pp. 25-26.

8. *Supra,* Note 7, p. 210.

9. *Ibid.*

10. Germann, A.C., "Changing the Police—The Impossible Dream?" (A Paper Prepared for the National Conference on Police-Community Relations, Western Center on Law and Poverty, Los Angeles, November 11, 1970), p. 10.

11. *Crime Control Digest,* May 28, 1971, p. 2.

12. President's Commission on Law Enforcement and Administration of Justice, *Task Force Report: The Police* (Washington, D.C.: United States Government Printing Office, 1967), p. 168.

13. Grimes, John J., "The Black Man In Law Enforcement: An Analysis of the Distribution of Black Men in Law Enforcement Agencies and the Related Recruitment Problem," An Unpublished Master's Thesis submitted to John Jay College of Criminal Justice, New York, August, 1969, p. 51.

14. Neiderhoffer, Arthur, *Behind the Shield* (New York: Doubleday & Company, Inc., 1967), p. 40.

15. *Supra,* Note 12, p. 196.

16. *Ibid,* p. 197.

17. Letter to the author from the President of The Hartford Guardians, dated December 20, 1970.

18. Letter to author from the President of The Hartford Guardians, dated December 20, 1970.

19. Goldstein, Herman, "Police Response to Urban Crisis," *Public Administration Review,* Vol. XXVIII, No. 5, (September-October, 1968), p. 420.

20. *Supra,* Note 4, p. 159.

21. *Supra,* Note 1, p. 31.

22. North City Congress, *Police-Community Relations Program Final Report* (Philadelphia, March, 1969), p. 86.

23. Waskow, Arthur, I., Report of a Discussion Conference Cosponsored by the Institute for Police Studies and the Center for the Study of Law and Society of the University of California at Berkeley, mimeo, no date, p. 1.

24. *Supra,* Note 7, p. 43.

25. Lindsay, *The Modern Democratic State* (London: Oxford University Press, 1959), p. 269ff.

26. The team policing model proposed here was borrowed from Professor John Kenney's article entitled "Team Policing Organization: A Theoretical Model," unpublished, no date.

27. Zwieback, Burton, "Democratic Theory and Community Control," *Community Issues* (Insitute for Community Studies, Queens College), Vol. 1. No. 4, (March, 1969), p. 11.

Institutional Racism and Crime Clearance

by Gwynne Peirson

One of the more successful, covert means by which white society has sought to maintain its dominance over blacks has been through the application of institutional racism. We are all more familiar with the day to day racism, the labeling of racial groups as being "different," less trustworthy, lazy, and less deserving of equal opportunities. By comparison, institutional racism is much more complex, and dangerous, having a wider impact on those toward whom it is directed.

Racism can be projected from two sources: Institutions and individuals. Individuals can band together and project racism from the institution they represent without any particular individual being involved in any overt act of racial injustice. It is for this reason that institutional racism is particularly dangerous. In addition to its more widespead impact on those it is directed against, the individuals who contribute to it can deny their own responsibility for racist practices. It is less overt and more subtle than individual racism. It originates in the practices of formally established bureaucracies in our society.

Basic to the history of institutional racism is the concept of "the white man's burden." White Americans popularized and adopted this concept of accepting the responsibility for looking after the affairs of "other races" in the late 1800's and early 1900's. In this view, white had a responsibility to educate the "poor colored masses" to adopt a better way of life.[1]

While the practice of institutional racism has existed in the United States from the time the country was first settled, the term appears to have been first coined by Stokley Carmichael and Charles V. Hamilton in their book, *Black Power*, where they made the following observation:

> Racism is both overt and covert. It takes two, closely related forms:
> individual whites acting against individual blacks, and acts by the total

white community against the black community. We call these individual racism and institutional racism. The first consists of overt acts
by individuals, which cause death, injury or the violent destruction of
property. This type can be reached by television cameras; it can
frequently be observed in the process of commission. The second type
is less overt, far more subtle, less identifiable in terms of specific
individuals committing the acts. The second type originates in the
operation of established and respected forces in the society, and thus
receives far less public condemnation than the first type.[2]

It is particularly within these concepts that there is a need to examine
and understand both the frequency and the purpose to which this tactic is
put by criminal justice system in the measurement and clearance of
crimes. The police, while representing the most visible segment of that
system, are only one of the systems practitioners of I.R. The police role has
been defined as the support and enforcement of the interests of the dominant political, social, and economic interests of the city, and only incidentally to enforce the law.[3] In practice, the police convert generalized racism
into specific racism. Their specific policies and practices of social control
mirror the racism of the dominant society which they represent.

It is not inferred, nor should it be believed, that the recognition and
acknowledgment of the existing I.R. is easily obtained. Much of the literature by those who have studied the police and police-minority relations has
had the effect of minimizing and clouding these issues. Many of the authors
who have studied these areas, e.g., Neiderhoffer, Wilson, Reiss, Bordua,
Skolnick, etc., have dealt with the racial aspect of police actions and
attitudes toward blacks, but at the same time tended to ignore and minimize
the racism which these practices indicate. Even in the matter of police
harassment, where innumerable instances have been proven, James Q.
Wilson has theorized that the increasing number of such complaints from
blacks might be attributed to the fact that "Negroes are being brought
under a single standard of justice; one reason for complaints of discrimination may be that the process is proceeding unevenly, and imperfectly."[4]
Wilson also suggests that such complaints against the police will increase in
number and in frequency, and attributes the expected increase to organizations competing for leadership "seeking out such issues in order to attract
followers."[5]

One of the more readily apparent uses of I.R. is in the use of crime
statistics to "prove" that blacks commit a disproportional amount of crime.
The official means by which we measure crime is in the hands of the
Federal Bureau of Investigation. Each year that agency publishes the
Uniform Crime Report. In a sense, this publication has become the "bible"
of law enforcement to show the amount, the increase or decrease, and the
geographical areas of the country where the most crime is committed.

The U.C.R. does not claim to know the total volume of crime, first because much crime goes unreported, and second because there is no requirement that individual police departments even forward their crime statistics to the F.B.I. The 1973 issue of the U.C.R. indicated that the total amount of reported major crime that year totaled slightly more than eight and one half million separate offenses.[6] Statisticians at the Justice Department have done numerous things with such statistics. They calculate how much each particular type of crime has increased or decreased each year, and the time of day or night each type of crime is most often committed. They have even been able to calculate that 16 serious crimes are committed each minute, that a violent crime is committed every 36 seconds, a murder every 27 minutes, and a burglary every 12 seconds.[7]

A major focus of the *Uniform Crime Report* deals with measuring the clearance rates of reported crimes. They take pride in reporting that 79 percent of all murders are cleared by arrest, that 81 percent of negligent manslaughters are cleared by arrest, and 51 percent of forcible rapes are cleared by arrests. These measurements go further, however. We are told which age groups are most arrested for specific types of crimes, and which sex is represented in these arrests. Predictably, we are finally told which races are represented in these arrests, including the percentage by which each race is represented in the total number of arrests for 30 separate criminal offenses, including the crime of "suspicion," which alone accounted for the arrest of over 13,000 blacks in 1973.[8]

It should come as no surprise that blacks are well represented in these statistics. According to the F.B.I., blacks accounted for 26.2 percent of a total of six and a quarter million arrests that year. Going into further detail, the *Uniform Crime Report* indicates that nearly 58 percent of all murders are cleared by arrests of blacks, 66 percent of robberies are cleared by the arrests of blacks, and 46 percent of all reported rapes are cleared by arrests of blacks.[9]

Representatives of both the criminal justice system and social service agencies use these statistics as a basis for hypothesizing as to why blacks as a race are so prone to crime. I have repeatedly been surprised at the numbers of scholars and professionals in the criminal justice field who unquestioningly accept arrest statistics as a measurement of who commits crime. Moreover, the manner in which the criminal justice system encourages the belief that its own statistics justify the belief that a highly disproportionate amount of crime is committed by blacks is institutionalized throughout the system, from police to prison.

The manner in which the *Uniform Crime Report* itself contributes to this belief is shown by the way in which they cease to measure disposition of persons arrested by race past the point of arrest. Racial statistics should be of primary importance throughout the measuring process, particularly since only approximately one third of all individuals arrested for serious offenses are ever formally charged with these crimes. Going back to the three types of crimes with the highest percentage of black arrests—murder, robbery, and forcible rape—we are dealing with offenses which have the lowest percentage of arrestees actually held for prosecution. Racial identification of those formally charged with the offenses would tend to indicate to what extent racism is involved in the arresting process. Since only approximately 25 percent of those arrested for murder are actually held for prosecution, and 27 percent of those arrested for rape and robbery are held for prosecution, insight into the degree that race is or is not a factor in the decision to prosecute would be available if these statistics were broken down by race.

There is evidence to indicate that the crime statistics, if broken down by race throughout the process, could be even more enlightening however. After indicating the percentage of those who are arrested who are also ultimately prosecuted, the U.C.R. also measures the percentage who are ultimately convicted and acquitted. These figures, again from the 1973 *Uniform Crime Report*, indicate that of the total arrests for murder, rape, and robbery, (114,044), less than 13 percent (14,554), are convicted of either the original charge or a lesser charge. What percentage of blacks arrested for these offenses are ultimately convicted? There is a strong suspicion that conviction rates for blacks are much higher than that of whites. We know that representation in prisons is grossly out of proportion. We know that of all persons who have been executed for forcible rape (455), blacks have represented 88 percent (405).[10]

If we were to measure disposition of criminal offenses by race at each stage of the criminal justice process, rather than merely at the point of arrest, a fair approximation of the degree to which race is a determining factor throughout the criminal justice system would be available. Such evidence is of primary importance in order to refute the allegations that "justice is blind," and the unsubstantiated claims that the crime rate among blacks is far above that of whites.

The manner in which racial arrest statistics are used to bolster arguments that blacks commit more crimes than do whites is graphically shown in one of the more widely read textbooks on the subject. The authors stated that:

> The general crime rate of Negroes exceeds the rate among whites. *The official statistics of arrest* [my emphasis] per 100,000 population of the same race 15 years of age and over for the entire United States, show that Negroes have arrest rates approximately three times that of the white population.[11]

The authors then go to state that "the rate of commitment of Negroes to state and federal prisons is about six times the white rate."[12] This pattern of using arrest statistics and prison commitments to "prove" the criminality of a particular groups is neither accidental nor naive. The time for treating accusations of racism by the criminal justice system, and more particularly the police, as unfounded allegations is past. The pattern by which blacks are assumed to be different ("different" meaning inferior and prone to crime) is apparent throughout the criminal justice system. The manipulation of crime statistics is both systematized and extensive. The evidence used by those who without evidence claim the black crime rate "exceeds the rate among whites" can also be used to indicate the selective process they use to justify their position, while ignoring the evidence which contradicts their argument.

Sutherland and Cressey, after using arrest statistics to bolster their position that the black crime rate is three times that of whites, then totally ignore their own findings that the prison commitment rate of blacks is about six times that of whites. Does this finding imply that blacks convicted twice as often as whites, or does it mean that they are twice as likely to be punished as are whites? The authors ignore these questions while choosing to discuss the rate by which they claim black crime rates exceed crime rates for whites for various offenses. As their method of measurement they used imprisonment rates, after already having noted the far greater likelihood that blacks will be sent to prison.

By commencing at the introductory stage of the criminal justice system— the police—it is possible to identify many of the factors which contribute to the imbalance in racial arrest statistics, and the uses to which these statistics are put throughout the system. Numerous studies have indicated that the attitude of the average white police officer toward blacks ranges from veiled dislike to open hate. As a result of his stereotyped opinions of blacks in general, and his indifference to, and lack of concern for their equal rights, he is inclined to use his official position to reinforce those views. Consequently, blacks are more likely than whites in similar situations to be stopped by the police on "suspicion." They are more likely to be arrested, and they are more likely to be insulted and/or assaulted (and coincidentally to become an arrest "statistic").

Typical of the racist attitudes which many white police officers project, and the manner in which they incorporate their racist beliefs into their occupational outlook, was an incident observed by a researcher who was conducting a study of the Nebraska State Police. The researcher was riding as an observer with a white State Police Officer, when the officer executed a sharp U turn and took off at a high rate of speed after a station wagon which was towing a small outboard motorboat on a boat trailer. After overtaking and stopping the car, the officer requested the occupants, two black men in their late thirties, to produce identification both for themselves and for the car.

After satisfying himself that everything was in order, the officer thanked the two men and he and his passenger drove off. While the officer was entering the event on his log he explained to the observer that "you seldom see a colored man with a boat," and therefore it was likely that it had been stolen.[13]

Not only did the police officer's explanation indicate that his judgment was based on the color of a man's skin, but that he was perfectly willing to back up his personal prejudice with the authority of his position. Acts and attitudes such as this are repeated throughout the country, varying only on how far the individual officer feels he can go before having to justify his actions.

Even the young white officers, who have not yet taken on the values and attitudes of older officers, and who are trying to do their job to the best of their abilities, are unwittingly involved in the results of those types of practices. As a result they experience what behavioral scientists refer to as "cultural shock."[14] The aggressive and militant hostility which blacks feel because of their being forced to accept the suspicion, hostility, and harassment of some white officers, is exhibited against the young officer. This tends to reinforce his latent attitudes toward blacks, and he then begins to act toward them as they expect him to, and as he sees the older, experienced officers act.

At this point the original prejudice has come full circle. Prejudice has begotten prejudice, and each side has acted as the other expected it to. Original prejudices have been justified in the eyes of the police, and their acts, which were the instigators of the whole process, are identified as "good law enforcement" by their superiors.

To many blacks, the ill-treatment and the brutality they have come to expect at the hands of the police, along with the powerlessness they feel in their attempts to make their plight recognized and acted upon, share in convincing them that the police are a racist institution. Others dispute this opinion, however. White institutions still attempt to rationalize and defend police actions however. The National Advisory Commission on Civil Disorders (The Kerner Commission) saw complaints against the police by minority groups as an indication that the police are in fact doing their job. In referring to complaints of police misconduct and malpractice (by minority citizens) the Commission stated that the complaints

> . . . may in fact be a reflection of professionalism; the department
> may simply be using law enforcement methods which increase the total
> volume of police contacts with the public.[15]

The ease with which complaints and charges made against the police are dismissed and disregarded by those in position to demand changes in attitudes and practices lends authenticity to the belief of many blacks that they are indeed a voiceless minority in demands for equal treatment at the hands of law enforcement personnel.

Arthur Neiderhoffer, a former New York Police official, and now a widely respected sociologist, sees cynicism as being at the core of police-minority problems. As a part of his concept, one must recognize that they— the police—have an organizational imperative that dictates that they act to negate criticism of them. To do this, Neiderhoffer claims, they produce a mass of statistics to validate their position, (to the police a large percentage of arrests of blacks "proves" that their suspicion of blacks is well founded) and attack the reputations and motives of those who criticize them.[16]

Neiderhoffer's observation that the police justify their actions by producing a mass of statistics points to the crux of the institutionalized racism involved in crime statistics. Even though the police need only make an arrest to clear a crime, they are the first to recognize that they cannot indiscriminately make these arrests. More and more, the average citizen is becoming knowledgeable as to his rights as a citizen, and to the constitutional restrictions on police authority. The police officer, therefore, is pressured into selectively choosing those to be arrested. All too often, those who the arresting officer feels are unable to challenge either his authority or his actions are selected for arrest or interrogation.

This selective process by the police was graphically shown in a study of the San Diego Police Department. One aim of the study was to evaluate the method by which San Diego officers determined that some citizens appeared suspicious and should be stopped for questioning. San Diego uses the Field Interrogation card system whereby each individual stopped for questioning, but not arrested, has his full identity recorded on an IBM type card which is then filed by the department. The researchers determined that of 20,000 cards filled out in a year's time, 80 percent were of blacks, who made up only about 10 percent of the city's population.[17] The fact that such a high percentage of interrogations by the police were of blacks would seem to verify the widely held belief that to the police, blacks are both legitimate targets of suspicion, and powerless to take action against the police use of them as a "crime statistic."

Although this and other evidence indicates racism within the police structure is widespread, white sociologists still attempt to minimize both its extent and its impact. William Westley found a *tendency* (my emphasis) on the part of white police officers to overestimate the extent of black crime. Additionally, when questioned as to the number of black officers on their departments, they constantly overestimated. Westley found this type of exaggeration to be both deliberate and defensive. He stated that it indicated a desire in white officers to disguise the truth whenever they perceive that truth as a negative reflection on themselves or their occupation.[18]

Another example of methods used by the police both to disguise evidence which tends to substantiate their racist tendencies and to justify the "criminal" statistic of blacks that have been killed at the hands of the police, was shown in a study of police killings in New York. In the late 1960's and early 1970's a four year study of killings by that city's police was conducted by the Metropolitan Applied Research Center. The intent of the research was to identify the race of persons killed by New York police officers, and at the same time to determine the race of the officers responsible for these deaths. Overall, the findings implied that over 75 percent of all such deaths were of minority persons, and that white officers accounted for more than 95 percent of these killings. The reason the researchers felt that their findings only *implied* these findings was due to the lack of cooperation they received in making their determinations. After the first year of the study the researchers discovered that throughout the remaining four year study the number of reports in which the race of the dead victim was omitted or "unknown" increased steadily, and that similar information on the race of the officers responsible for the deaths decreased proportionally.[19] It is likely that the officers involved in these deaths (or those officers responsible for reviewing such reports) both understood and appreciated the implication that a highly disproportionate number of white officers were responsible for an equally disproportionate number of deaths among minority persons.

Even with this mounting evidence of institutional racism within police law enforcement, most white researchers still choose to deny or minimize its existence. In one such study, Bayley and Mendelsohn attributed some of the police racial problems to the fact that "generally Negroes and Spanish-named people have not been attracted by police careers and until recently have not been encouraged to seek them."[20] The authors were possibly naive in assuming that the mere presence of minorities on police departments would decrease or eliminate the racial prejudice of white officers, but the manner in which they changed history by stating that ". . . until recently [blacks and Spanish-named people] have not been encouraged to seek them [police careers]" rather than acknowledging that for many years it was both legal and socially acceptable to prohibit these people from gaining employment as a police officer, and that this prohibition was based solely on race.

In examining and measuring the extent of racial prejudice on the part of white officers, the authors found that police to be racially prejudiced, "but only slightly more so than the community (in which they worked) as a whole."[21] The criteria used to determine prejudice is in doubt, since Bayley and Mendelsohn first indicated that only 3 percent of their sample indicated a "dislike for Negroes," and yet they followed this by pointing out that 50 percent of the officers questioned felt Negroes were pushing too hard for their rights, and about 33 percent felt that blacks do require stricter enforcement procedures than do whites.[22]

In an overt attempt to minimize the reliability of charges of police brutality and harassment toward blacks, the authors pointed out that policemen give little credence to charges of unfair treatment by them. Although the department in which they conducted their study was said to have 23 black officers, there was no evidence that any of the black officers were interviewed. Rather, in several instances the views allegedly held by black officers were voiced and interpreted by white officers. In a further example of white officers overestimating statistics when they see the actual figures as being detrimental to their image, the authors noted that 88 percent of the 822 white officers on the department stated that they had worked with a black officer. The question of how 733 white officers could have worked with 23 black officers was not explored.

One of the most extreme uses of institutional racism involved the killing of citizens by the police, and the methods by which these killings are justified. It is very seldom that a killing by a police officer while on duty is found to be unjustified to the extent that the officer is charged with a criminal offense. In the late 1960's Northwestern University conducted a study of killings committed by Chicago police officers over an 18 month period. The lengths to which they found authorities would go to justify a killing by a police officer was indicated by a case in which a white officer responded to a report of a woman being raped. When the officer arrived at the apartment where the reported crime was believed to be taking place, he heard screams and sounds of a scuffle coming from the apartment. In order to gain immediate entry, the officer claimed he fired his shotgun in an attempt to shoot the lock off the door. Instead, he killed the woman (black) who at the time was attempting to resist her attacker. The Police Review Board determined that no criminal charges should be filed against the officer, but did recommend that he be required to report to the police gunnery range for retraining in the use of his weapon.

The matter of citizens being killed by police officers does not receive the public attention that killings of police officers do, in spite of the fact that killings by the police are several times higher than the number of killings of police. The Uniform Crime Report devotes several tables to the measurement of assaults and/or killings of police officers. The report contains no statistics on killings by police.

Professor Paul Takagi of the University of California, in a study published in 1974, noted that while the rate of police killed has remained fairly constant, the rate of killings by the police has risen steadily over the past decade. Moreover, Takagi's findings showed that black men have been the victims of these killings at a rate nine to ten times higher than the rate for white men.[23]

In examining the racial discrepancies, Takagi noted that, in 1964 for example, black males constituted 28 percent of all arrests, while black deaths at the hands of law enforcement officers made up 51 percent of all killings by the police. Law enforcement officials are prone to argue that blacks have a higher representation in arrests for the major crimes of homicide, rape, robbery, aggravated assault, burglary, theft, and auto theft. Supporters of this position contend that the black involvement in these offenses is at a higher rate than their rate for all arrests, and since supposedly most citizen killings result from these major crimes, the black death rate is not out of proportion. To contradict these allegations, Professor Takagi noted in his study that in two of the years covered, black arrests for these major crimes ranged from 30 to 36 percent.[24]

Another typical argument which was refuted by Takagi's findings dealt with the often heard claim that the reason so many blacks are killed in confrontations with the police is that more black "criminals" are found in the violence prone age group where "desperate" criminals are more likely to be found. Takagi also studied the age groups where "desperate criminals" are least likely to be found, the very young and the very old. In studying deaths caused by police of citizens in the 10-14 age group and of citizens 65 years of age and older, Takagi found that:

> In proportion to population, black youngsters and old men have been killed by police at a rate 15 to 30 times greater than whites of the same age.[25]

Earlier we referred to the success which white society has had in maintaining its dominance over blacks by the imposition of institutional racism. The police constitute the most visible and legal expression of that society. As the police have struggled for their own middle-class status they have become willing participants in continuing efforts to intimidate those who challenge practices which are aimed at inhibiting blacks and other minorities in their efforts to gain equal access to opportunity and reward. What has long been defined as a "Negro Problem" must be re-examined and acted upon. The results of such a re-examination was perhaps best expressed by Knowles and Prewitt, who stated:

> Just possibly the racial sickness in our society is not, as we have so long assumed, rooted in the black and presumably "pathological" subculture but in the white and presumably "healthy" dominant culture. If indeed it turns out that "the problem" is finally and deeply a white problem, the solution will have to be found in a restructured white society.[26]

REACTION

Do you see any way that a group such as this can impact on the Uniform Crime Report and definition to those reports?

Peirson: I would think that if as a group, we were able to bring more widespread recognition of the fact that they drop the question of race immediately after the point of arrest and that this is a major weakness, that it could possibly be incorporated. From year to year they change their format—putting things in and leaving things out. It's common practice, but they have never dealt with race past that point of arrest. And it serves the system, it serves the system very well to further enforce the idea that the arrest is the important statistic.

I think it's a deliberate attempt to justify the discrimination in criminal justice process. You often hear people say "if he wasn't guilty, he wouldn't have been arrested."

Davenport: When you look at the whole concept of institutionalized racism and crime clearance what does it lead you to conclude?

Peirson: First, the perpetuation of the system; the need of the system to justify itself. They need these statistics, they need to be able to point to some group and say that this group is responsible for a great deal of our problems, and I think that our need first and most importantly, is to be able to understand these games and to be able to deal with them.

For example, the observer program—ride-a-long with police—now this type of thing is good if the people doing the observing understand the system. If you're riding with a policeman, you can't expect to hear over the radio "I got a bad nigger on the corner." You're gonna have to understand what the radio code is. It will mean the same thing. But you've got to understand what is happening in order to deal with it, just simply sitting there and watching what's going on isn't enough. So we need to fully understand each segment of the system in order to be able to change it.

Murray: The UCR was organized by the police for the benefit of the police and of the system. They merely attempt to report incidents reported to the police and are susceptible to all kinds of manipulations. People report out of the department information coming in to the extent that it serves the interest of the department. If the chief wants to look good, he may want to do it the other way around when he's seeking more money in his budget.

I think if we are looking for perhaps a clearer picture of what's going on, I think the mood has to be toward collecting statistics on some broader kind of a basis than placing responsibility for the collection, verification and analysis in the hands of somebody who perhaps is a little bit less biased or who has less of an interest in bias than to change the outcome of the system.

Perhaps the information should be collected by somebody other than the police and perhaps it could be analyzed and used by somebody who's not a part of the system at all. It seems to me that there are valid needs and justifications for that information to be in the hands of the consumer, if you want to view us as consumers of the system. There is a valid need for that information in the hands of those who are elected lawmakers, there is a valid need for it for every citizen who's paying taxes. It's now viewed as a need and an instrument of the police end of the system. I see that information as something that's of value to the entire society.

Boone: I want to go on record as being very very worried about the retrieving of any kind of data about black individuals. Why do we need this kind of data on blacks, juvenile delinquents or adult persons?

I read this morning that some white organization has out of one hundred thousand blacks, compiled a who's who of ten thousand people, and I hope I'm not in that book. Considering the power of the CIA and FBI they may get that book and allow any nut to knock us off.

Peirson: My main concern is not so much that we have our own system of measuring. We have been the victims of interpretation of what the existing statistics mean. Other people tell us what they mean. White social scientists, white criminologists tell us what arrest statistics mean, and we need to understand how they're gathered, what they actually mean so that we're not victims of their interpretations.

Davenport: Why do you believe the professionals, the criminologists, the sociologists, who are writing in the field, who really have the benefit of a lot of information that's been published from a black perspective, choose either to ignore, minimize or not to understand the one way or restrictive nature with which they view the data?

Peirson: There has not been that much information published by blacks because we don't get the moneys to take off a year or two and write while someone pays our salary. In addition, I think it's apparent that these people have benefited by the system, they have become what they are. They have gained the ranks or the recognition that they have by the existing system. The Skolnicks, Neiderhoffers, Wilsons, all of these people have a vested interest in maintaining the system as it is because the system perpetuates their rank and their recognition. Colleges and universities are making it difficult for blacks to receive any recognition in criminal justice.

Davenport: To what extent, is what James Q. Wilson and the others are doing—a reflection of the whole Harvard Syndrome of protecting their kind of class structure, their kind of power structure. To what extent is it reflective of something else? Because you know, it's one thing if it is the protection of their power. It's something else, if it's doing something else.

Brown: I think we have to realize that research is not value free. Of course, we may have a scientific method of gathering data, but the values of the individuals doing the analysis also come out. I mean that's where the problem is. The white researchers going to research on black people, they're doing it on the basis of their own perspective which is white. It's very significant, it's really through being concerned about influencing public policy that we have to begin and start publishing our research if we're doing research or things of this nature, so that we too can influence public policy.

At this particular point, those who make public policy only have the perspective on which to base their decisions. I think that's what's essential to keep in mind that research is not value free, that biases are inherent in research like anything else.

Fattah: I think that another instance of this problem relates to a study done by Dr. Miller who came from Harvard into Philadelphia, did a study on the gang problem, and didn't talk to one gang member. He talked to agencies that dealt with gangs, but he did not talk to a single gang member. We realized that the summary in that report was incorrect. As a response, sampled five hundred gang members and had former gang members interview current members asking some of the same questions that Dr. Miller asked. We had a press conference to announce our findings. Only two reporters showed up, so the brothers took our reports to every TV, radio and newspaper office in Philadelphia.

Cindy Sulton: I think this is bringing something out very clearly. That may have been, you may have gotten that report to the local television stations, but I never heard of your report and I have read Miller's report and Miller's report is probably the one that most blacks and most everybody is going to read. There has got to be a mechanism established where your report actually gets printed. Equally as important, if you ask the people around the room who have published what journals they've published in, I think we'll find that they aren't the journals that are widely read, because of the way that these articles are reviewed by journal committees. All of the professional associations have their journals and the way they decide what gets printed and what doesn't is again your buddy system. And until we can do something about that, we have to publish in their journals, and we have to make them let us publish in their journals.

Woodson: I shared Miller's paper with Jimmy Hargroves and Charlie Gilliam who are both gang intelligence workers for N.Y.C. Jimmy says with the limited resources they have there are fifty-five gangs that they have not been able to gather information on. I don't know how the hell Miller could come in, spend two days in New York and write about the gang problem.

Charlie Gilliam: Miller's report talked about the fact that the number of gang killings in Los Angeles exceeded that of New York City. He does not go on to explain, however, the classifications which vary from department to department. That's the bottom line—L.A. may decide that a killing by five or more people is a gang death.

Davenport: During the time that India was struggling for freedom from England, Ghandi decided that rather than contest their system of justice, he chose to ignore it. What that meant was that when Indians were charged with crimes, they'd walk into court, without lawyers backing them up to challenge their arrest. They said in effect that the English had no jurisdiction over them, and refused to participate in the system. And when that happens, the system breaks down.

In this context, what I suggest is if we have a question, as to the legitimacy of the research, then even with the Harvard mentality, if we use the League as a resource, the other systems will break down. I think one of the major functions that the League could serve would be to disseminate information. There's a lot of resourceful people at this conference who could be used through the League as a conduit to verify this information or discredit it for use.

REFERENCES

1. Louis L. Knowles, and Kenneth Prewitt, editors. *Institutional Racism in America* (Englewood Cliffs, New Jersey: Prentice-Hall, 1969).

2. Stokely Carmichael, and Charles V. Hamilton. *Black Power: The Politics of Liberation in America* (New York, 1967).

3. Joseph Lohman, and Gordon Misner. *The Police and the Community* (Berkeley, California: University of California Press, 1966).

4. James Q. Wilson. *Varieties of Police Behavior* (Cambridge, Mass.: Harvard University Press, 1968).

5. *Ibid.*

6. The major crimes are identified as "index offenses," which include murder, forcible rape, robbery, aggravated assault, burglary, larceny-theft, and auto theft.

7. *Uniform Crime Report for the United States—1973* (Washington, D.C.: U.S. Government Printing Office, 1974).

8. *Ibid.,* p. 133.

9. *Ibid.*

10. Ramsey Clark, *Crime in America* (New York: Pocket Books, 1970).

11. Edwin H. Sutherland and Donald R. Cressey. *Principles of Criminology, Seventh Edition* (New York: J.B. Lippincott Co., 1966).

12. *Ibid.*

13. Jack J. Preiss and Howard J. Ehrlich. *An Examination of Role Theory* (Lincoln, Neb.: University of Nebraska Press, 1966).

14. James S. Campbell, Joseph R. Sahid, David P. Stang. *Law & Order Reconsidered* (Washington, D.C.: U.S. Government Printing Office, 1969).

15. *The National Advisory Commission on Civil Disorders* (Washington D.C.:

U.S. Government Printing Office, 1968).

16. Albert Neiderhoffer. *Behind the Shield* (New York: Doubleday & Co., Inc., 1967).

17. *Op. cit.* Lohman and Misner. *The Police and the Community.*

18. William Westley. *Violence and the Police* (Cambridge, Mass.: MIT Press, 1970).

19. *Police Killings* (New York: Metropolitan Applied Research Center, 1972).

20. David H. Bayley and Harold Mendelsohn. *Minorities and the Police* (New York: The Free Press, 1969).

21. *Ibid.,* p. 144.

22. *Ibid.,* p. 163.

23. Paul Takagi, "A Garrison State in 'Democratic' Society," in *Crime and Social Justice* (School of Criminology, University of California, Spring-Summer, 1974).

24. *Ibid.*

25. *Ibid.,* p. 30.

26. *Op. cit.,* Knowles and Prewitt, *Institutional Racism in America*, p. 4.

Prison Construction Moratorium: Its Relationship to Crime Prevention

by John O. Boone

Last August I was privileged to be an expert witness in a class action suit in Federal Court, essentially a motion for the right to treatment for prisoners incarcerated in Alabama's penal system. Presiding was United States District Judge Frank M. Johnson. Judge Johnson played a key role during the sixties in the process of adjudications for civil rights. For me his presence over this prisoners' rights case was an omen. The prisoners' rights movement developed prior to the civil rights movement, flowing from a rash of prison rebellions that peaked in 1953. During the eighteen months from April 1952 through September 1953 there were about thirty prison rebellions, or other major disturbances, more than had taken place in the entire preceding quarter century.[1] Then, as is the case now, prisons were managed under the philosophy of keeping them quiet at all cost. Austin MacCormick coined the phrase, "paregoric prisons." He said, "Prisons of this type are run on the principle of what I once called paregoric penology, remembering the old remedy for keeping bothersome babies quiet."[2] Public indifference and political intrigue during this period promoted mediocrity and political appointees, cronyism and nepotism, underpaid guards who went about the job with the idea that a good prison is a quiet prison, and often they were willing to work for very low pay for the opportunity to "work niggers." As long as there are no escapes, no disturbances, nothing to draw unfavorable publicity, they do not care that the prisoners are drifting along on a low physical, mental, and moral condition and that most of them will leave prison worse off than when they entered. Behind the prison rebellions were:

1. Inadequate financial support and official and public indifference.

2. Substandard personnel.

3. Enforced idleness.

4. Lack of professional leadership and professional programs.

5. Excessive size and overcrowding of institutions.

6. Political domination and motivation of management.

7. Unwise sentencing and parole practices. [3]

The rebellions created an atmosphere of revolution in prisons. I have indicated that it is my opinion that the prisoners' rights movement predated the civil rights movement. It is remarkable that the items of prison maladministration listed above are similar to the attitude of political, social and economic forces that were behind the rebellions in the cities during the sixties. Eric Hoffer has observed that, "When a population undergoing drastic change is without abundant opportunities for individual action and self-advancement, it develops a hunger for faith, pride, and utility. It becomes receptive to all manners of proselytizing, and is eager to throw itself into collective undertakings which aim at showing the world." [4] After the rash of prison rebellions that climaxed in 1953, a revolutionary atmosphere engulfed prisons. There was a push for litigation; notable use of remedies against injustices occurring during confinement through injunctions, habeas corpus writs, and civil suits for damages. Although these means were inadequate to precipitate great changes at the time, they produced actions in connection with the right to counsel and decisions against certain limitations of the right to practice a religion, particularly in connection with those prisoners who embraced the Nation of Islam. At Atlanta Federal Prison I often observed black men who had embraced the Islamic faith straighten up from a position of shuffling and bowing and head scratching and look prison officials squarely in the eyes as men after the contagion of the revolutionary mood and temper were generated in the aftermath of the rebellions of the early fifties. I saw this same mood in the eyes of the masses as they sang "We Shall Overcome" during the throes of the revolution in the free community during the sixties. So Judge Frank Johnson's presence in the Alabama prison case was an omen.

A moratorium on prison construction is a legitimate means of securing the postponement of prison or jail building programs. Hopefully, by effective use of moratorium programs, society will get used to the idea and public administrators will come to appreciate the movement and begin to pursue good alternatives. Personally, I hope that the moratorium will result in decreased dependence on imprisonment as an important component in the criminal justice process. My experience indicates that for most of the prisioners the tendency to return to prison, once they have served a sentence, is not affected by the length of the sentence except that institutionalization probably decreases one's ability to adjust in the free community. There is much evidence that release from prison with supports makes a difference in the rate of return when one compares the success of individuals with support to the success of individuals that had no supports.

It was a happy day for me to see the prisoners at the Draper Correctional Center demolishing the punitive isolation unit at Draper Prison in Alabama, known by inmates as the "doghouse." I had testified the day before that the unit was the worse that I had ever seen in the country. The doghouses were an array of about ten small one-man cells. The cells were encased in a solid concrete building with one steel door. No guard was on duty. When the door was opened for me, the stench hit me in the face, and the temperature seemed to be about 105 degrees. I was convinced that someone had to be dead in that punitive isolation unit as I heard groans from more than one man. Five young men, all under the age of twenty, were piled into the first two one-man cells that contained, of course, no furniture. In the first dark hole one young white man was placed with five black men. In the second, the hole contained one black man with five whites. The function of this arrangement calls for very little imagination by one who has watched the antics of crude custodial officers over a period of several years. Of course, only one toilet hole was available and when I wondered what happens when more than one person needed to use the toilet, the custodial manager that accompanied me said, "I have only one toilet at my house." Judge Johnson ordered the doghouses demolished and I am certain that their abolition makes very little difference on the incidents of bad behavior in prisons. Three months after I became superintendent of the Lorton Correctional Complex (the prisons for adult male offenders of the District of Columbia) located in Lorton, Virginia, there was a demonstration in which prisoners burned the punitive segregation unit. I did not have it reconstructed for the purposes of punitive segregation and it made no difference. Later on I directed a social worker to make a survey of the frequency of trips to punitive segregation by individuals to determine if the experience had any value at all other than a degree of deterrence, in the sense that others might be wary of experiencing punitive segregation. The findings indicated that the use of this kind of maximum security made no difference at all in the rate of return, or frequency of exposure to the unit. For some, on the contrary, a sentence to the hole was a badge of honor and established a reputation of being "tough."

At the Massachusetts Correctional Institution in Concord, Massachusetts, I arranged for the demolition of a one hundred year old prison. I was able to do this with part of a two million dollar grant which I had received from L.E.A.A. for the purpose of depopulating the Concord Prison. The prison wing was empty in less than three months after the project was begun. Funds were used to support the prisoners as they reentered the community for work, training, or education. Research recently published by the Massachusetts Department of Corrections indicates that the rate of return for the men and women who were released during the time of my tenure, 1972-1973, is under twenty-five percent for those who were released with help as they endeavored to adjust and become reintegrated in the community, much lower than those who were released without any help at all. A few years ago at a meeting at the Ford Foundation on correctional program policy and planning, Sheldon L. Messinger presented a two-page paper advocating that the government pay states and other localities that would agree to demolish prisons, with the provision that ex-prisoners be used on the demolition teams. At the time, I considered his presentation a joke. Now, with the rise of the moratorium movement, it turns out that this is a good idea. As a former practitioner and prison administrator, the most influential volume of theoretical studies for me was Pamphlet 15 of the Social Science Research Council, theoretical studies in social organization of the prison published in March of 1960. Time does not permit me to abstract this work in this paper, but it will be helpful if I share with you an observation of three of the social scientists that compiled one of the studies for the Social Science Research Council.

> We have drawn a picture of the inmate social system as a set of interlocking roles that are based on conformity to, or deviance from, a collection of dominant values; and we have suggested that these values are firmly rooted in the major problems posed by the conditions of imprisonment. The maxims of the inmate code do not simply reflect the individual values of imprisoned criminals; rather, they represent a system of group norms that are directly related to mitigating the pains of imprisonment under a custodial regime having nearly total power. It is hoped that this view of the prison opens fruitful lines of inquiry, which may lead to better understanding of the social structure and functioning not only of prison populations but of social groups in general. Although many theoretical and empirical issues are left unresolved by our analysis of the inmate social system, three problems seem to be of critical importance.

> 1. There are questions concerning the possible relationships between the various argot roles found in the custodial institution, on the one hand, and the social and psychological factors on the other. Do certain roles tend to be associated with a particular personality structure? And if so, does the personality structure influence selection of the role, or does the role tend to create the personality type? What influence is exercised by age, religion, previous criminal record, present sentence?

> 2. How is role playing in prison related to the individual's behavior outside the prison? . . . We can attempt to discover how alienation,

exploitation, and cohesive behavior within the walls are associated with similar patterns of behavior in the free community.

3. The relations between group values and changes in the social environment should be examined more fully. If the environment is made less rigorous, will group solidarity receive less emphasis? Given the officials' task of maintaining custody and internal order, is it possible to break down the suspicion and distrust of the conforming world embedded in the inmate code?[5]

Sheldon Messinger made his proposal for the demolition project for the nation's prisons more than ten years after participating in the development of the theoretical studies in the social organization of the prison. We can assume that he has come around to the position of advocating the abolition of prisons. After trying multiple programs in prison, many based upon the ideas that I gathered from the theoretical studies, I have come around to the position that prisons should be abolished. A moratorium on prison construction is a strategy that could help us to move toward this objective. Unfortunately, it is always necessary for me to state that my position for the abolition of prison does not mean that I believe dangerous people should not be contained. It means that prisons are colleges that produce criminally dangerous people.

The most impressive effort to effect a National Moratorium on Prison Construction is the joint venture of the National Council on Crime and Delinquency and the Unitarian Universalist Service Committee. The N.C.C.D. issued a policy statement calling for a halt to institutional construction in favor of community treatment, April 25, 1972. The objective of the National Moratorium is to seek sound, systemic alternatives to incarceration. I must point out that while I endorse the National Moratorium, both as a member of the board of N.C.C.D. and as one who has observed the heavy use of prisons for more than twenty years and has been convinced of their fruitlessness, that nothing short of an honest assault on the social and economic injustice that generates criminal behavior can prevent crime. In a great sense liberal reformisms are just as menacing for the black community as incarceration. As we consider a moratorium, then, and other programs that could result in change in policy, we must be prepared to replace the old policy with solid programs. This will be extremely difficult because policy planning and implementation is dominated by American and European social scientists and practitioners. The prevailing theology which dominates research and theory in criminology is liberalism. It is the liberals who dominate the field—writing the most influential literature, serving as government consultants, staffing local and national commissions, working in Think Tanks, working as researchers for the Congressmen and women, and acting as brokers for large agencies and foundations. There is considerable disagreement among these social scientists. Some are conflict theorists, others are labeling theorists, and there are the traditional positivists. But, as a rule, they are unified by their common ideological functions.

In coming to a discussion with the aim of examining black perspectives on crime and the criminal justice system in America, there is a need to make clear some general definitions of the issues involved. Fortunately, I am already limited in that my concern in this paper is the ramifications of a moratorium on prison buildings. But, I want to point out, that this symposium arrangement can provide a base upon which a synthesis may be generated out of which policy could develop. Whether the national political administration turns over or not, blacks, in my opinion, must become involved and must insist on input into national criminal justice planning and policy development or sit in an Ivory Tower and watch neighborhoods and communities die. The letter of invitation indicated that the symposium is to be based on the research conducted by black criminologists in the area of black on black crimes and the impact of the criminal justice system on the black community, and input is to be drawn from a selected group of criminal justice practitioners. I have suggested above that the current crisis of accountability of criminal justice agencies can be placed at the feet of criminologists and criminal justice administrators who suffer of a white orientation. Hopefully, the brothers and sisters of the discipline of criminology have avoided the traps that are set by their counterparts of the other world, the world of sociology or the American Sociological Society, where, I fear, too many individual sociologists are living off of their sociology. In this symposium we need to wonder if individual sociologists can be depended upon to be scientific, or should we be practical as we evaluate both social scientists and social welfare administrators, realizing that we are dealing with human beings who are both hungry and ambitious and must be concerned about their own breadbaskets. We want to know if those who dominate positions of research, planning and policy development and implementations may be induced to use their research to arrive at predetermined conclusions. Frankly, we need to determine if they can be purchased with fellowships, grants, and other profits. We need to be worried about the extent that government special interest groups and philanthropic foundations favor or reject certain people because of predetermined notions about their point of view. For us these questions are crucial, particularly in view of the large new pool of revenue, which is less than ten years old, by L.E.A.A. amounting to 800 million dollars in 1976. The question is, do black scholars and black practitioners have an even chance at fellowships and grants for criminology and criminal justice projects.

Another issue concerns the discipline of the presenters which reflects on their notions about the nature of crime and corrections. Hopefully, we have economists and educators joined with us in this symposium of criminologists and criminal justice practitioners. For example, a historian would be valuable as we assess total black experience in this country. A multi-disciplined approach to policy planning and development is needed in the pursuit of a better perspective of crime and corrections based upon an analysis of the whole black experience.

Dr. Larence Reddick talked about this in a symposium at the Harvard Center for Urban Studies, June 7, 1974, on black education and public policy. He was getting at the insidiousness of the publication, in October of 1972, of *Inequality* by Christopher Jencks, assisted by others—according to Dr. Reddick, many others. Dr. Reddick said, "Some of us were alarmed by the sophisticated scholarship that this book represented and the cleverness with which its assault upon the education of black and low-income children was wrapped up in a package of pseudo-liberal reform."[6] Clearly, according to Dr. Reddick, the Jencks' volume was not a product of a loner, but rather a corpus, almost a conspiracy, that planned and plotted its charts and extrapolated curves in regular meetings for several months in succession, including one of its moving spirits, Dr. Daniel Patrick Moynihan,[7] who had made use of the statistics of social disorganization to write the most devastating attack yet made upon the black family, and went on to become Chief Advisor on Social Policy to two successive presidents of the United States and, remarkably, of two different political parties. This collaboration formulated machinery that was mounted with the objective of formulating public policy. Reddick pointed out that the Harvard-M.I.T. group succeeded in getting itself well located and funded and, in addition to its projection of a half dozen books, enlarged its advisory to institutions and public officials and took over the quarterly, which is ironically named *The Public Interest.*[8]

My thesis is that blacks are shortchanged because they have limited input into policy planning and development. I am a living example of the dangers that blacks face when they come into positions of power, too often effective use of the power is either blocked or the position is lost.

The Federal Bureau of Prisons secured the passage of the Rehabilitation Act of 1965 and had the authority to depopulate prisons and establish credible programs in the community, including the authority to contract with state and local governments and private concerns. At the time that this legislation was passed, the Federal prison system consisted of thirty-six facilities. Essentially, the act authorized the Director of the Federal Bureau of Prisons to extend the limits of the prison into the community for various reasons, including any reason which is consistent with the reintegration of the prisoner into his community. This was a policy that could have been used to enable the Federal Bureau of Prisons to get out of the prison business and assume a leadership role in relationship to state and local communities through entering into contractual arrangements, setting standards, and otherwise watching the "rehabilitation" of Federal prisoners that could have been helped in facilities closer to the community. The late F.B.I. director, J. Edgar Hoover, interfered with this thrust of the Federal Bureau of Prisons to fully implement the Rehabilitation Act of 1965, after the then new director of the Federal Bureau of Prisons, Myrle Alexander, made statements about his plans to use the new legislation to enable prisoners to maintain community contacts, particularly the idea of enabling the prisoners to foster healthy relations with family and others in the personal environment to which he or she would eventually return. In this instance, a law enforcement leader became involved in preventing corrections from doing its job.

The idea of a prison and jail moratorium was brought to my attention when I was superintendent of the Lorton Correctional Complex. It was developed then as a notion to reveal the hypocrisy of the system that, in the opinion of the advocates, could not live with a heavy use of jails and prisons, calling the prisons the nation's poorhouses. The point was that the State needed prisons because the system was unable to provide jobs for a large segment of the society, particularly blacks and lower-class others. I had just emerged from a rebellion when the idea of jail building moratorium came to me. I decided to make full use of the Rehabilitation Act of 1965, which at the time was applicable to the Federal City, the District of Columbia, and I allowed most of the prisoners to go into the community for work, training, education, and furloughs in order to maintain and reinforce family and community ties. The black director of the District of Columbia Department of Corrections, Kenneth Hardy, was trying to make full use of his authority and develop education, training and work programs for the men and women from the District of Columbia. Ability to do this at Lorton was facilitated by virtue of the fact that the prison was located about twenty miles from the community. His efforts to develop a humane and helpful correctional process were fought by the Southern congressman that controlled the District committees for several years. Ken Hardy was compelled to call a moratorium on the programs that I developed at Lorton because a group of powerful officials joined together to question its legality. They did not deal with the fact that the programs were effective and that morale had gone up at the prison and that men were motivated for work and education and training, and enthusiastic about another chance to become responsible citizens. Their position was that what John Boone is doing is illegal.

Unfortunately, at the time, the President of the United States, Richard M. Nixon, felt overwhelmed by the students who were storming into Washington alleging that we were involved in an undeclared war in Southeast Asia. The peace movement often resulted in mass jailings and it required all of my energy to stand in front of the prison door and prevent the detention of students at the prison under my charge. The President was also concerned about his pledge to reduce crime in the District of Columbia. He directed key Justice Department officials to develop legislation for pretrial detention and the ability to enter homes without knocking. Those officials joined together to stop the rehabilitation/reintegration programs that I had developed included some judges, Chief of Police Jerry Wilson, Department of Justice officials, the White House, and some powerful congressmen. The *Washington Star* published a story that the Washington, D.C. Police Department was reducing the value of stolen property, thereby reducing possible felony offenses to misdemeanors, as a means of impacting the crime rate in Washington to suit the design of the President of the United States. Even at that time in 1972, the President showed a proclivity for bringing crime off the street into the White House.

After Ken Hardy placed a moratorium on the reintegration programs that could have resulted in depopulation of the prison and reduced the need for prison space, I decided to resign. Soon afterwards I was appointed Commissioner of Corrections for the Commonwealth of Massachusetts. Finally, I was to be in a position of power, policy making, and policy implementation. Ironically, in that I was inclined to insist on honest decision making, I was to stay in the position for only eighteen months, three days and three hours. During the last three hours of my incumbency I was in a confrontation with the Governor and the Secretary of Human Services, Peter Goldmark, who had developed a dramatic plan for my dimissal and sacrifice on the altar of politics. In Massachusetts, a powerful prison guard union with a very strong political base, and some liberals who did not like my imprudent style, through subterfuge and outright sabotage had placed me in a position to become a political liability and this literally stopped prison reform in Massachusetts.

Currently, in my opinion, the same kind of forces are joined together to place in disrepute the potential of rehabilitative, skill and educational programs that might be developed in the correctional process. These forces take the shape of social scientists, public administrators, and some who could be classified as nothing more than charlatans, setting themselves up as experts (penologists) providing fuel for use by persons who want to secure crime control bureaucracies particularly the heavy use of prisons. For example, opponents of busing and school desegregation found a new fuel for their arguments in the public comments by James S. Coleman. Those who want to continue to make very heavy use of prisons find fuel in the arguments of Dr. James Q. Wilson of Harvard as well as in such well meaning reports as that of the Committee to Study Incarceration and even in Senator Edward Kennedy's proposed legislation for a mandatory two-year sentence for violent Federal crimes; proposed legislation which is misleading in that it did not acknowledge that already very long Federal sentences are meted out to persons who commit the kinds of crimes identified in the bill. Let's take a brief look at the kind of fuel that is often espoused by Dr. Wilson:

> The purpose of isolating—or, more accurately, closely supervising offenders is obvious: whatever they may do when they are released, they cannot harm society while confined or closely supervised. The gains from merely incapacitating convicted criminals may be very large. . . . If much or more serious crime is committed by repeaters, separating repeaters from the rest of society, even for relatively brief periods of time, may produce major reductions in the crime rates.[9]

I learned last week that Henry Tiger has been released from prison in Arkansas. He was an eighteen year old first offender several years ago who was caught stealing property from a local department store. The court gave him ten years plus one year consecutive for trying to escape from jail. After going through degradation processes which involved jeering, prisoners saw him as a "turkey" and someone that they would take advantage of, he escaped from the maximum security prison in Arkansas and was free for five years. He told his employer in Arizona that he was a fugitive. For five years he worked, paid taxes, and supported his new wife and during the last two years of his freedom, his child, until the F.B.I. arrested him as a fugitive. He was returned to prison facing at least ten years and had he been required to serve that length of time, keeping him in prison even in Arkansas where trusty's are still used in various and sundry roles, cost the taxpayers seven thousand five hundred dollars per year per prisoner. Had he been required to stay in prison for ten years the cost would have been seventy-four thousand dollars. In Arizona, his wife was eligible for one hundred seventeen dollars a month, which amounted to one thousand four hundred and four dollars per year, and had she remained on welfare in eventuality of her husband's imprisonment, would cost taxpayers eleven thousand and forty dollars. I present this story as an example of the nonsense that taxpayers suffer as a result of the foolish, ineffective use of expensive incarceration. A final word or two about a moratorium on prison construction. Because the prisons have been neglected so long, programs for correctional change can take many forms. One approach is to focus on the shortcomings of the institutions in the hope of finding more immediate relief from intolerable conditions. The lack of adequate medical treatment and decent food, the maintenance of healthful and sanitary living conditions, the menial nature of prison industry's programs, the dehumanizing nature of prison routine, the use of drugs in large amounts to pacify prison populations, the voided rights of prisoners, censorship of mail, and restricted visiting rights are all potential issues. Another approach would be to focus on the development of meaningful programs for prisoners; programs of work and educational releases, furloughs, and vocational training. But, as a recent decision in the Alabama prison suit has shown such approaches beg the question. Alabama was ordered to make tolerable the living conditions in its brutal prisons, prisons more appropriately defined as warehouses for black men and women. The state was ordered to provide each prisoner with the opportunity to participate in programs of work and education designed to assist his or her re-entry into society. The court declared that confinement to an Alabama prison actually makes the prisoners worse, debilitates them and makes them less able to successfully re-enter society. The initial reaction of Alabama officials was that sufficient State funds to make the court ordered improvements simply did not exist, there wasn't enough money to make the prisons even modestly acceptable. Nevertheless, the State's financial problem could not block the court's decision. If you keep people in prison, you must care for them. This situation is not exclusive to Alabama. Any state ordered to make its prisons habitable would face the same problem, and every state prison system is a candidate for such an order. But the fact is that there simply is not enough money to make the institutions work. Therefore any program for correctional change which does not strike at the heart of the prison business, at the institutions, is a flight of fantasy and an invitation for more trouble. A moratorium program then, based on the assumption that institutions can and must be closed, is worth supporting, even if such an approach merely establishes a prisoner's right to treatment and care and begins to educate the public that his is an insatiable desire for revenge and vengeance.

Moratorium programs must develop the ability to find out from the public how much punishment and vengeance it can afford. The construction, construction financing, and maintenance of jails and prisons proved to be extremely costly. Planning and site acquisition are costs frequently ignored in calculations. The building of new jails and prisons now costs from $25,000 to $50,000 per bed. Debt service is expensive, often costing more than the actual construction. Maintenance costs now average at least $3,600 per bed per year and frequently cost much more. Building programs often involve rip-offs of the taxpayers. In Massachusetts I observed a two prison building where money was stolen from the taxpayers. Specifications for institutions called for six inches thickness of concrete. The structure was constructed with a little more than one inch with a hollowness in the center that certainly represented the cost of concrete that went into somebody's pocket. Steel and concrete industry represents a lobby as powerful as the Rifle Association to fight the retention of the prison business.

Prisons became the most important component of the country's penal system a little more than 200 years ago. This is the Bicentennial Year, the 200th birthday of the country. More than two years ago, as mentioned above, I closed the East Wing of the Correctional Institution in Concord,

Massachusetts. This wing of the Concord prison had been brand new during the Centennial in this country 100 years ago. In recent years there had been more rebellion in that prison than there had been in the town of Concord at the start of the Revolution. Concord Prison was built twelve years after Lincoln's Emancipation Proclamation, which supposedly marked the end of bondage for three million black prisoners. When I closed the East Wing of the prison 35% of the people housed there were black, while less than 3% of the six million inhabitants of Massachusetts are black. This affluent, historic New England community can boast the fact that a native son, Ralph Waldo Emerson, was one of the few people to support John Brown and his little army of liberation at a time when most white liberals like William Lloyd Garrison condemned the insurrectionist action. Yet, more than 100 years later one can count the number of black families residing in the town of Concord on ten fingers. It is also remarkable that during this the Bicentennial Year, the threat of an enfranchised prison population caused the free people of Concord to abandon their attitudes of apathy and complacency as they turned out in hordes to vote after a prisoner announced that he was going to run for public office in the community where he was incarcerated. Analysis reveals the dishonesty in the criminal justice system reinforces tendency of selection of blacks and Puerto Ricans and chicanos for the heavy penalties of the criminal justice system. A look at the percentage of blacks in the general population of a state and the percentage in prison population makes a point. In California the percentage of black people in the state, including chicanos, is 18%. The percentage of blacks in prison population is 50%. The percentage of black population of Florida is 15.3%. The percentage of black prisoners is 55%. The percentage of Illinois state population of blacks is 12.8%. The prison population is 53% black. North Carolina's black population is 23%. Its prison system contains 55% blacks. Texas has a black population of 14%. Black prison population is 44%. Alabama's state population of blacks is 26%. The black prison population is 60%. Pennsylvania's black population is 8%. The percentage of blacks in prison population is 50%. Clearly prisons have been used for something other than the containment and control of crime.[10]

In conclusion, President Lyndon B. Johnson, in an address to the nation on July 27, 1967, in a response to his commission's report on violence said:

> . . . The only genuine long-range solution for what has happened lies in an attack—mounted at every level—upon the conditions that breed despair and violence. All of us know what those conditions are: ignorance, discrimination, slums, poverty, disease, not enough jobs. We should attack these conditions—not because we are frightened by conflict, but because we are fired by conscience. We should attack them because there is simply no other way to achieve a decent and orderly society in America. . . .[11]

It is my opinion that we do not need attack. We need honesty, for so long we have been hoodwinked by crash programs and crisis-oriented commissions. What is needed is an honest piece of the action, no matter who is governing, conservative or progressive, we want no more and no less than what we are entitled to as citizens of the United States of America. In this symposium, hopefully, we will determine ways and means of getting this point across to the general public as well as the powerful decision makers. In addition to the right to treatment of the prisoners there is need for another model, an economic model. People leaving prisons return to their communities to find little more than economic oppression, governmental neglect, heavy police control, no jobs, no resources, and a quick trip back to prison. In this sense, prisons are instruments of genocide for individual groups and committees. Considering the increasing population of black men and women in prison, a case can be presented that would characterize imprisonment in the law enforcement-criminal justice process as an instrument for their extermination. Consequently, if a moratorium against prison building means that it is a strategy for abolishing the heavy use of prisons, the movement should not only be taken seriously, but it should be taken over by black leadership who would be ready to make credible recommendations for real programs that could contribute to the health and decency of the communities where black people live in large numbers.

REACTION

Lamb: What kind of impact do citizen groups or individuals have? Do those who are concerned about prison conditions make visitations there, do they meet with the administrators, and meet also with the residents in the prisons? What kind of an impact does this have, or what suggestions could you make?

Boone: The potential is great. That kind of activity (prison talks and visitations by concerned citizen groups or individuals) now is done largely by white people, especially white women. They go there to try to find a black man and unfortunately they go there, I would suspect, to put the milk bottle in the prisoner's mouth. I don't believe in that. At Lorton, I want them turned on, you see, to get excited and get angry. The worst thing in the country is to have the kind of federal prison which looks like Holiday Inn. And, you can't even get angry, you know, it's so good. Black people should develop the strategy of going into prison. You've got instruments, you can go in there now, and if you can't you should insist on it, to register voters. We ought to get in those prisons and say, "Hey, we want to teach the brothers how to vote, where they live, in Attica, and make a big case, hey we're going to vote."

Ward: In New York, I can't tell you much of any place else, the jails are in worse condition than the prisons. Herman Schwartz, the first government appointee in the history of the State of New York, was not confirmed by the Senate and all he did was to ask that New York State jails come up to the minimum standards that New York State prisons already had. For that, he was deemed a wild-eyed radical who could not be tolerated by the Sheriffs of the State of New York. They drummed him out of the corps and Gov. Hugh Carey refused to withdraw his name, and he was not confirmed. So that's the condition in New York; the jails tend to be older than a hundred years.

I live in Albany. They are celebrating their *tricentennial* for the City of Albany and the jail was there then. If you pass a law as they recently passed in New York which says no more arrests for public intoxication, the jails are just as full now as they were before because they now add trespassing or loud and boisterous and drunk and that circumvents the laws so that they'll fill up the jails just as well.

There are some strategies that are being studied by our department in an effort to do something about that in conjunction with the corrections commission. One of the things that we would like to do is to try to shift that population back towards urban settings. The jails are in the urban settings and the cities are bankrupt, the state is almost bankrupt, but they have greater resources than the cities and perhaps by funding some state dollars into city facilities, we can upgrade those prisons, and at the same time, do something about shifting populations back towards the cities. It's a very, very difficult thing to do.

Prisons are a big business and people make their living at prisons. The village in Attica would not be there if there were not a prison to support it. It's a very important industry in that town. The volunteers are white, middle-class ladies, and a lot of young ones at that. You see more interracial relationships in prisons than you'll see any place in the City of New York, and, of course, that's more than you're going to see any place else in the State of New York.

Young white girls come to prison and they develop those relationships in prison, and you'd be amazed at what you see there in terms of young white girls—all volunteers, from the colleges and from the communities. They come in and they help. There are also a lot of young white male lawyers and female lawyers who are there helping. But, it's the young whites who are the volunteers that come into prisons in great numbers and cause a lot of problems with the guards because they get very upset about it.

The other thing that Boone said about the moratorium on prisons: he frequently talks about the abolition of prisons and you get a lot of objections on that immediately. Objections even from myself as an administrator, if you talk about closing down prisons tomorrow, I know there are a lot of people in prison now who I'd be damned scared of if they were outside here. I don't know what to do with them. I wouldn't trust them with the nice lady from Philadelphia (Fattah) either. I'd be afraid for her, right now, with some of them.

But there are a lot of prisoners who don't belong in prisons, and prisons are a kind of self-fulfilling prophecy: as long as you have them, you will find people to put in them, and that's what's happening in many of the states. We're going up at about a rate of 20 percent all over the country. New York is exceeding that by some percentage points, and if you look at what's happening in the last several months here in New York, you will see that three major alternatives to incarceration, by way of diversion programs, have been closed down in the last few months, and those people are winding up in Rikers Island.

Foremost among the people who come into the state system are those who had been in residential treatment programs for drugs. These programs, for all practical purposes, have been abolished. Those people will come into state prisons as judges find that they have no alternative. They don't have the alternative of putting them into a drug treatment program. They won't let them 'plea down' to the lowest felony level, or the misdemeanor level. They'll keep them at the higher level and put them into prison, if those prisons are there.

So that, if you don't begin to think about a moratorium on prisons, you will really be providing spaces, or providing a place for a judge to send people. And then, you get a large constituency that supports that, because once you build that prison and provide all those jobs, those people will come out and really beat the drum for you.

The biggest support I had for the largest prison that I've opened in New York City this year was from the employees who were going to lose their jobs if I didn't put a prison at their place. And they came out and they supported it, and we have a prison there. I think New York has to move into a moratorium on prisons and I certainly support John Boone in that, because the goal that you set will really control a lot of what you do.

I'm reminded of Kennedy's attempt to reach a decision on reaching the moon, and he called the cabinet together, and he said, "I'm going to say that we will put a man on the moon before the end of the decade," and one person said, "I think I can improve on that." And, the President was surprised; what he said was, "I think we ought to say we're going to put a man on the moon and return him." And, the man who said that was the first man to walk on the moon. You know, that's a hell of a thing when you think about it, because it's a lot different than putting a man on the moon; putting a man on the moon and returning him. All you need is a great big gun to shoot him up there, and you don't have to worry about getting him back.

That has got to be what you think about, that's what John is talking about with prisons, too. You're not going to abolish them this year, but if you don't start thinking about stopping, stop building them, then you're never going to start thinking about alternatives, and you will close down the diversion programs like court employment and two other large ones.

You will not think about what's going to happen with those people and what's going to happen is that they're going to go into prison, which wouldn't be bad, it wouldn't be bad, and I would support it if prisons did any good. But, we all know they *don't* do any good. So, we're supporting something that isn't going to do any good. One thing that you can be certain about prison is that you turn out a better and more professional criminal than you sent in.

Lamb: I'm still concerned about this; you indicated the positive impact that citizen participation has in humanizing the prisons. I'm concerned with the fact that you have indicated that most of this interest is with white middle-class women, and I was just concerned with the reason for the absence of blacks. Archibald indicated that this is a great deal due to the fact that blacks perhaps don't have the leisure, or they don't have the means of getting to these far-out places, but it seems like something that we should look at.

Boone: I'm scared to even go by a courthouse in Cedar Town, Georgia, especially I'm afraid to go by a jail. I'm scared of policemen. White ones. And, furthermore, I'm embarrassed because you're not supposed to go to jail. When my nephew was in Vietnam, he was in and out of jail because he sniffs glue and all of that. He's a nice guy. He didn't rob anybody. But I didn't tell anybody that he had gotten into trouble. I was embarrassed.

My nephew was killed on Peachtree Street, and I'm a big civil righter in Atlanta. He was killed, a great big guy. I can remember when he was called in front of his grandfather, a big AME minister, and he was laughing. Will Boy, shot, and me and my brother didn't say a mumbling word. Now, that's an indictment on myself. They killed Will Boy. They beat him up, eight policemen, and put him in jail. He died there. I didn't say anything. He was middle-class.

Brooks: I would like to reiterate, and especially to the women who are sitting here, that I was a nine hour-a-week volunteer in Trenton State Prison. It's not easy to be a volunteer in a prison; it's not an easy thing to do or see. But, I am disturbed about the fact that there are no black women in those prisons, and going in there on a daily basis means a lot, but even if you can give only three hours a week, it's important.

I'm also concerned that there's no foundation funding the training, or assisting women to go into the prisons. I wanted to go to Dannemora or Stormville. It would take a day, and if I'm a black woman, more than likely, I don't have a day. But if somebody were to finance, for instance, the bus trips to enable sisters to go to the prisons and do things like write letters for the prisoners, it would help a lot. And, sisters, if you're wondering where our men are, that's where they are, in prison.

Now, the white girls are smart enough to go in there and look them over, and I'm not joking about this. White women go in that prison and work their cookies off getting brothers out on work releases, taking them home to bed, and you complain about the fact that we don't have any men in our community, because all of our energy is inside that prison.

I'd like to speak to those ladies who work with LEAA programs, and say to you, maybe you should go back and organize to get some young women who have time and nothing else to do, to do something as simple as cook. I got ten mothers once in New Jersey to do this, cook up big pots of food and take it into the prison.

Now, the Muslim women go in. In some communities, the Muslim women go in to these prisons every single day and bring special food to the Muslims because you know in the prison, they don't make any attempt to address the religious needs of black folks, only rabbis.

Ward: In New York, they do.

Brooks: Well, in New York, just rabbis, right?

Ward: Rabbis and Muslims.

Brooks: Not in Washington, D.C., and a lot of other places. Now, for years, I've been looking for some organizations, and I've even gone to people like Dorothy Height (of the National Council of Negro Women), and said, "Listen, Dorothy, I'm interested in working with some young people to get them going." I didn't get anything. Nothing. I haven't gotten one nibble about that on a personal level.

If you're working with young women, or if you're around young women, and you want to do something worthwhile, then you walk into the prisons. You'll see some of the healthiest, most attractive, bright young brothers in our black community. You ask them what they are doing there. I can remember a 22-year-old, gorgeous, and he said that he's doing 15 years. He's lifting weights all day, and he's not taking drugs. The white girls are in there getting them, and they come in damn near naked, too.

Boone: Let me say something to the women. I attended a conference last year that the LEAA gave for Dorothy Height and a bunch of garden club women. They called it "Hands Up," and the LEAA had given them $400,000. (It was a federation of women's clubs.)

The first question I heard off the floor from a little old white lady was, "How can we stop the furlough bill?" Now, $400,000. There were a few blacks there, about ten women. Now, we ought to be out looking for some LEAA money to do another kind of program.

Murray: You are urging a moratorium on construction and the ultimate abolition of prisons. You've had an example in Massachusetts of an attempt on a smaller scale to close juvenile facilities. What has been the experience and what does that teach us about the likelihood of success of an abolition movement for adult institutions?

Boone: I sort of referred to it in the beginning by saying that administrators are careful because it could backfire. In Massachusetts, they are reinstitutionalizing. The judges again are calling for secure things. Now, if you move far enough, they can't turn around. I've got a new law, which as the federal law, extends the limits of the prison into communities with the long-range objectives of getting some of the money.

I spent $34 million dollars last year, but it was on guards' salaries; guards' sophisticated unionization starts off with $9,000, but if the inmates should start a riot, the salary goes up to $15,000 a year. So, that's where all that money went by March. I had an objective of putting that money in Rockville's multi-service center, and Umoja kinds of things over a period of time, so the possibility of the moratorium on not building any more prisons, is to get the people out on their personal recognizance from jail. Let's contract, and let's keep non-dangerous offenders out, and let's ask the community how much punishment and vengeance is possible.

I want to say that we have to realize that in regard to prisons, all of us are in prison to a certain extent. Don't just look at the one million people in prisons, or jails on one day because burglar bars are going up all the time, and most blacks now live in sort of minimum security. I think that what I said in the beginning holds true.

We've got to be involved, and raise the level of political sophistication. We talk about money, we talk about policy, but what we've got to do is teach that middle-class black person who he really is. We are all conservative and want to put inmates away. Yet, some of these people can begin to come out and cut the prison population in half. If I had been able to cut the prison population in half in Massachusetts, that would have been $15 million dollars, $15 million dollars in the black community! So, from one community to another, you need to think about that as a strategy.

REFERENCES

1. Austin H. MacCormick "Behind the Prison Riots," *The Annals of the American Academy of Political and Social Science,* Volume 293, May, 1954, p. 17.

2. *Ibid.,* p. 22.

3. *Ibid.,* p. 24.

4. Eric Hoffer. *The Ordeal of Change* (Harper and Row, New York, 1967), p. 3-4.

5. Gresham M. Sykes and Sheldon L. Messinger. *The Inmate Social System* (Social Science Research Council, 30 Park Avenue, New York, March, 1960), p. 19.

6. Lawrence Reddick. *Social Scientists and Public Policy,* Temple University, June 7, 1974. Unpublished.

7. *Ibid.*

8. *Ibid.*

9. James Q. Wilson. *Thinking About Crime* (Basic Books, Incorporated, Publishers, New York), p. 173.

10. National Moratorium on Prison Construction. 2215 M Street N.W. Washington, D.C.

11. Report of the President's Commission on Civil Disorders, July 29, 1967.

REPUDIATION OF REHABILITATION AS AN OBJECTIVE
OF THE CRIMINAL SANCTIONING PROCESS

Williams v. *New York,* decided by the United States Supreme Court in 1949,[21] probably represents the high-water mark of judicial acceptance of the treatment philosophy in the criminal sanctioning process. Since that time, and particularly during the last ten years, rehabilitation has gone under a cloud. It is now being attacked from all quarters as an impossibility and, further, as a positive evil, vesting in authorities powers over the individual which are both tyrannical and far beyond the scope of their competence.[22]

Numerous studies have been published to show that rehabilitative treatment programs, whether conducted inside prisons or outside in the community, have never demonstrated their superiority in effectiveness[23] over alternative penal measures or pure custody without rehabilitation.[24] Proposals are heard to abandon rehabilitation as a primary goal of the criminal sanction—retaining it as a supplementary goal offered on a voluntary basis —and to return to short, fixed and determinate sentences.[25]

This movement against enforced rehabilitation has within an amazingly short time received the official recognition and blessing of the federal government. In two recent speeches[26] Norman A. Carlson, Director of the Federal Bureau of Prisons, attacked the medical model of criminal corrections, admitted the non-rehabilitative effect of coercive treatment measures, and announced his support of the idea of relegating rehabilitation from its position as a goal of punishment to that of a resource available to inmates on a take-it-or-leave-it basis. In one speech[27] he said:

> In corrections we have developed what many people refer to as 'the medical model' for handling of inmates. When an offender comes into the prison system medical terms are used to describe the kind of services he gets. He is examined and tested, he is put under 'observation' by a 'treatment' team, his problems are 'diagnosed,' and then the therapy and treatment is 'prescribed' to cure him of his criminality.
>
> People who use such language have conveniently overlooked the fact that the vast majority of offenders are not sick, either physically or mentally. The incidence of mental problems among inmates is no higher than it is for society as a whole.
>
> The cause of crime cannot be disguised as though corrections personnel were doctors looking for tuberculosis or psychiatrists examining a patient for mental illness. *We cannot prescribe with precision what's wrong with the criminal and then lay out a course of treatment to bring about a cure.*
>
> Until the psychiatrists, the psychologists, and the behavioral disciplines can give us clearer, fuller explanations of what motivates the

offender, *we are going to have to live with the fact that we can't change offenders.*

All we can do is offer them encouragement to change themselves. We can do this by creating a climate in our institutions that helps inmates when they have made the decision to rehabilitate themselves. Our role must be facilitative not coercive. We can offer them, as we do now, a wide-ranging program of counseling, education, work, vocational training and a variety of other services. It is up to the inmates themselves to take advantage of these opportunities.

We are certainly not kidding the inmates when we talk about re- habilitation and treatment. They know we don't know how to rehab- ilitate them. They simply go along and play the game, for the most part. So it's time we quit kidding ourselves, the press and the public. As Norval Morris says in *The Future Imprisonment*, people cannot be rehabilitated against their wills. Rehabilitation must be voluntary to be effective, and the medical model used in corrections over the years is fatally flawed.

These remarks were not made "off the cuff" by the Federal Director of the Bureau of Prisons. There clearly has been a change of official policy and these speeches are testing the public reaction to it. This is revealed by the fact that, in his June 19, 1975, message to Congress regarding legislative proposals for the control of crime, President Ford underplayed or ignored rehabilitation and stressed the deterrent and incapacitative functions of imprisonment.[28]

One of the President's proposals was for mandatory minimum sentences for certain federal crimes (aircraft highjacking, kidnapping, and dealing narcotics) and for many repeat offenders. While this recommendation does not represent a total repudiation of rehabilitation as a goal of punishment, it does indicate a drift away from compulsory rehabilitation and the in- determinate sentence in favor of fixed sentences designed to maximize the deterrent and incapacitative functions of criminal punishment.[29] In fact, concurrently with the release of the President's message, Justice Department officials explained ". . . the purpose [of the recommendation re: manda- tory minimum sentences] is to stress deterrence by demonstrating that a convicted offender has virtually no way of avoiding prison through suspended sentences or probation."[30]

In an earlier address made on April 25, 1975, at Yale Law School to the Yale Sesquicentennial Convocation Dinner, the President previewed many of his later recommendations to Congress and the thinking behind them. Here also he stressed not only the deterrent, but also the incapacitative, function of imprisonment.[31] No mention was made of rehabilitation or of improving treatment facilities in federal prisons or elsewhere. It is clear that the omission was deliberate. All that the President said with regard to the treatment of felons in prison was that ". . . convicts should be treated humanely in prisons. Loss of liberty should be the chief punishment."[32]

Once it becomes official doctrine that "prisons do not rehabilitate," "that we cannot diagnose what is wrong with criminals or prescribe effective treatment measures," or that corrections should be "facilitative, not coercive," the justification for the sentencer's consideration of information which relates *solely* to the diagnosis of the offender's "problem" preparatory to classification and assignment to the appropriate treatment regime disappears. If the offender is free to accept treatment or reject it at his discretion, then clearly the sentence cannot be based on information which relates to the correctional measures which will provide the offender with the most effective programs for his reformation, since he is free to reject them wherever he is sent or whatever is done with him. This would seem to be as true in the case of correctional measures provided in the open community as it is of those provided in prison institutions. When, to boot, this information is prejudicial to persons of minority races or of low socioeconomic status, then it becomes more than useless; it becomes positively harmful and unjust. Those who could most benefit from rehabilitative efforts are now likely to escape exposure to them as they diminish in importance and availability within the prisons. Is this a new and even more insidious form of institutional racism, this turning away from a treatment philosophy?

Covert racism is no longer practiced within the prisons. Society has moved from blatant racism to a form which is more settled and pervasive because black inmates are unable to identify directly those persons who are responsible for their suppression.

Prisons are still administered by a white staff, and those who lead the custodial staff are generally all white. Yet, those who are punished the most severely are black inmates. They are now being placed in special units which have various names such as Readjustment Unit, Adjustment Center, etc. These special units are designed to allow correctional administrators to deal with prisoners who are seen as "trouble makers." Rubin "Hurricane" Carter was placed in such a unit in New Jersey because he was perceived as a trouble maker in the system. How long must we wait until blacks are placed in responsible decision making positions within the correctional system?

Covert racism may take the form of assignments within the institution. Whites generally are given the choice assignments within prison walls, or racism may raise its ugly head in custody classification. If an inmate is given a custody which prohibits his movement within the institution, then he is excluded from most programs because of that custody.

Not only must we be concerned with crime in the black community, we must also be concerned with the offender once he is convicted. Ninety-eight percent of all offenders return to the community. If we are going to reduce crime, we must work with that offender, and also with the correctional administrators to reduce the tensions that exist within the institutional setting.

CONCLUSIONS

The prisons as they exist today will continue to breed persons who are sophisticated in crime unless fundamental changes are made. These changes must be administrative as well as programmatical. To say that rehabilitation has failed, and that the choice will now be made by the offender as to which programs they should be involved in, is abdicating the responsibility of the state to try to bring about change.

We as black people must begin to question the motives behind such permissiveness, especially since black people are now the majority of offenders within prisons in the United States.

REACTION

Sullivan: I would just like to add to that in addition to our attempts to redefine crime, I think we need to redefine rehabilitation. What are we being rehabilitated from? Are we being rehabilitated from stealing because we need to steal, are we being rehabilitated from a mental illness? I mean, just what is rehabilitation as well as what is crime?

The second thing I'd like to say is that my recent research, which came out in the form of my dissertation, was conducted within three Philadelphia Country jails and one Pennsylvania State institution, Graterford, and the dissertation was on the effect of the Nation of Islam upon the present inmate culture. It focused on the idea that black people are suffering from social, economic and political marginality, which necessarily affects the ego identification of black people, and we are particularly degraded when that marginality is exemplified in enforced incarceration.

The Nation of Islam, which I conceived as a politically conscious reference group, going into social psychology so to speak, attempts to cope with that marginality by supplying, number one, a sense of belonging, and also by supplying a positive ego identification.

Now, we view rehabilitation traditionally, prior to our redefining it. I have to say that my research suggests that the Nation of Islam is the only rehabilitative agent, the only one in the institution, which provides reeducation. Number one, it offers an awareness of the greatness of our predecessors and our societies prior to our exposure to the United States in the early fourteen or fifteen hundreds. Number two, it provides reeducation about the strengths of black people because of their ability to survive racism and oppression in this country. Through these two mechanisms, the Nation of Islam has instilled a feeling, for inmates, of self worth.

Murray: I wonder if I see a paradox when you mention the Rubin (Hurricane) Carter case in New Jersey. When the paper argues for rehabilitation, if it means before your redefinition, then rehabilitation as most of the people administering prison systems intended, tends to expect the inmate to admit that he did whatever it is he was charged with doing. He accepts now whatever has happened to him and he goes through some kind of religious experience or something.

At the basis of it all is the assumption that in the end a person is going to say, "I'm responsible." How does that fit in with a situation like the Rubin Carter case in which the guy says, "I didn't do it?" So, to argue for rehabilitation in his kind of case, strikes me as a paradox in that the defendant gets stuck there in a "Catch 22" situation forever.

Brooks: But isn't the whole purpose of prison expected to be the ultimate in behavior modification in this society? If we assume, for instance, that most blacks are in prison because they have challenged the system, then we have to accept the fact that their rehabilitation to the prison community and to the American community at large has meant, "I am going to make you behave the way I want you to behave and to accept my value system as the only one that's valid."

What scared people the most about Rubin Carter's situation is that he would not accept prison. He would not conform to the minimum expectations. He refused to have his wife visit him in prison because he rejected his whole presence there. So that moving Hurricane Carter out was inevitable, because as long as he was there, he was a symbol of the system's lack of validity.

Rehabilitation has always meant, "I'm going to make you behave the way I behave or the way I think is important," and we know who's in charge of that process.

Boone: I would like to say that in my first job in corrections at Walden, the New York State Training School for Boys, I believed that if the prisoner didn't admit that he was guilty, then he didn't get rehabilitated. Incidentally, while I was at Walden, Claude Brown, author of *Manchild In the Promised Land,* was incarcerated there.

Later, when I went to Atlanta, I started with the belief I'd held earlier, but then I changed over a period of time. I would ask an inmate, "Are you guilty?" More than likely, he would say, "No, I'm not guilty." Now, I know that not only Hurricane Carter, but the average black inmate—and white inmate, too—will not admit that he is guilty, and I've tried to understand what they were saying. I think they were saying, "I'm not guilty because I'm in a bind."

And, I want to say one thing about your notion about redefining rehabilitation. I think that's very important. I think that we ought to pursue either another model, or redefine rehabilitation to invoke an economic model into the rehabilitation model.

Carmichael: I would go one step further. I think that rehabilitation simply means that the inmate never returns to prison, and that quite often we measure rehabilitation in terms of recidivism rate: how many people return to prison; and that, in fact, rehabilitation has no functional meaning. It's simply measured in terms of how many people return to prison, and if a number of people are returning to prison, then rehabilitation has failed.

Sullivan: See, rehabilitation could mean that you learn how not to get caught. I mean that could be rehabilitation for us. Just how do we steal without getting caught? People steal legitimately every day. Is it the task of rehabilitation to train people so that they're elevated into positions where they can commit white collar offenses? We have to determine what kind of crimes we're talking about. What are we rehabilitating people from?

Napper: I just have a question in regard to Dr. Sullivan's dissertation and this whole conception of rehabilitation. What criteria did you use to establish the fact that the Nation of Islam was an effective rehabilitation agency?

Sullivan: Just by interviews, questionnaires, and my own personal experiences with the prisons.

Napper: Was a follow-up done on people who were released from prison?

Sullivan: No. No.

Napper: Was this in respect to their own view while they were in the prison system?

Sullivan: Yes, while they were in the prison system, given the fact that some could certainly be jailhouse Muslims, in terms of just not wanting to be raped, or wanting five suits of clothing for a week as opposed to one per month. But, no, there was no follow-up because of obvious time constraints.

Ward: I support Dr. Debro's view on rehabilitation because I think he has discerned that there is a concerted movement towards eliminating rehabilitation. It never has achieved a substantial amount of funding in any prison system that I'm aware of, and if you think back prior to Attica, in

New York State, there was practically no money spent on rehabilitation, and prisons were relatively inexpensive because everybody was locked in at five o'clock in the evening.

Now they're out until 10 or 11 o'clock, and if you get rid of rehabilitation, or even the reasons for rehabilitation, prisons will become very inexpensive to operate again because we will lock everybody in probably at five o'clock. What would be the purpose of letting them out if it's not to engage in rehabilitation programs?

So, given a lack of rehabilitation, I think the whole concept of rehabilitation can be argued more on the basis of providing a humane environment inside the prison, and less concern about whether or not this man ever engages in crime, because as long as the standard becomes recidivism, you can't win that battle anyway.

Now, how am I going to be responsible for a young guy who's in there in his early twenties, and I'm supposed to be responsible for him until he's in his late sixties. If he should ever commit a crime anywhere between the time he's in prison, and the time he dies, then the system is said to be a failure. That's an unrealistic standard. A large part of prison is doing time and how do you get from seven o'clock in the morning until seven o'clock the next morning, and it's much easier to do it doing somehing than it is doing nothing.

Boone: How much would it cost you, Ben, to provide humane treatment or care?

Ward: Well, it's costing in fiscal year '76-'77 about $11,200 to do what we're doing now. I can tell you that it would cost substantially more to do an effective job in caring for prisoners if people really cared. Training would be provided that would prepare a person to make a living on the outside.

Now, there are several definitions of recidivism, but I just wish that a black academician would begin to identify a standard and goals which set three years, or as in the case of New York State, where you must be under parole supervision for five-and-a-half years. I would even accept that. The people who operate prisons would then be compelled to accept some responsibility, or to do something for those in their charge. But, it's unrealistic to expect this, given the selective enforcement policies of the police. We must begin to deal with the problem at its basis, and that is, with juveniles in the black communities.

Brooks: When people have been in institutions most of their lives, this naturally has some effect on their ability to adjust, or not to adjust, to life on the outside. Why can't we identify these young people earlier?

Ward: Yes, I can't answer those questions for New York State because allegedly the juvenile records in the state are confidential, and are not available to the sentencing judge, although they are readily available to others in the system. How they can be made available, and how many case records are available, is a very difficult thing to determine. If Arch Murray who is here knew the sentencing judge had access to juvenile records, his people would be creating an uproar in court. So that there is some evidence that they do get a hold of the records, but it's hard to say in which cases.

Brooks: All right, in New Jersey, there was a study done, and the information was released, and they said that about seventy-five percent of the current prison population had been institutionalized since they were about twelve years old. In other words, their whole lives had been a succession of being sent to one juvenile institution after another. And, of course, the judge seemingly is not influenced by that, as you say, but it is interesting that these inmates have become lifelong institutionalized people, and it certainly has to affect their latest sentence.

Ward: Just one comment on that. Forty-two percent of the new incarcerations in New York State are first-timers into a state corrections system. In New York State, the Family Court is such that it's pretty difficult to get yourself into a secure facility in the state as a youth. You get into a lot of other things, but you don't get into jails and prisons.

Napper: I was going to say that the apparent lack of commitment to rehabilitation in any sense is very apparent when you consider that even if a person is able to use, as one criterion for rehabilitation, the acquisition of some occupational skills, many of these occupational skills require a license to practice. However, once a person is released from prison, he or she is prohibited from acquiring a license, if you've been convicted of a felony, which raises a whole other problem about reentry that I guess should be a concern of ours, it emphasizes the lack of commitment to the whole concept of rehabilitation.

Sulton: I was going to say on the question raised about people who were institutionalized for long periods of time, that I've been involved in a scientific study for the Department of Corrections in Washington, D.C. As a result of this, I was going through the records of individuals in prison, and in those files were contained their juvenile records. Now, nobody has gone through since that law was established that those juvenile records are supposed to be expunged and taken out of the record. They're there and they're going to stay there. But, in looking at those records, I saw that a number of the people who had, indeed, been incarcerated in what was the

National Boys Training School Division, were in there for the first time for neglect. They were welfare cases. The second time they were in for something else, and they were back and forth, for welfare and criminal acts. Later, they were in and out of the adult system.

Murray: That's not true in New York. Although I don't know if the pattern of recidivism is any different, the fact is that the law in New York is so old that those records don't appear in the case folders of inmates in New York. It only makes it more difficult to arrive at probably what would be the same conclusion that she (Sulton) found. But, you just can't find a juvenile record as part of the inmate's current file.

Now, there is a way to get them. There's no doubt about that. For instance, I defended a person in a federal court action in which the New York City Police Department was a defendant. We were suing because the police were making juvenile records available to people who should not have those records, and it was done routinely. Nobody even thought about it. Yet, juvenile offenses are not in the folder just routinely here in New York State, and they have not been for many years.

S. Fattah: In terms of long-term incarceration, there must be some type of sub-culture for persons who know that they are going to spend a large part of their life in confinement. Have there ever been studies or anything like that done on prison life for persons serving long sentences?

Sullivan: Yes. There have been a few studies done by white criminologists. It would definitely say that there are roles, just as we have in our society. You have to remember, though, that they're working within the confines of a structure, of a building, and then an organization that is not visible; the formal organization of prison administration and policies.

In answer to your question, yes, there have been studies done on the inmate culture regardless of length of incarceration, but I don't think that they're generally applicable to black folks.

Boone: I have known whole families to have gone to jail; they grew up in the training school, just as she (Sullivan) said. I organized some of them according to their gangs, used any kind of model, anything, and they developed community counterparts and transmitted their culture in prison. There is a man named Don Clemmer, incidentally, who came up with the term, "prisonization," which is similar to socialization. He thought that the longer you stay in prison, the more you do become institutionalized, and you have values, roles, and language. I think that a black social scientist should take a hard look at that for us. Like she said, whites are the only ones examining this.

S. Fattah: The reason why I mentioned it (whether studies had been done on prison life for long-term inmates) is because it seems that if given that type of situation, where the type of thing is going on, and ones who are just there for short periods of time would have to start relating to this lifestyle. I know that somewhere in there then there has to be something that would make it more difficult for these inmates to deal with their problems while incarcerated. Studies may be able to determine whether problems are presented to these individuals who are incarcerated for short periods of time because of whatever long-term lifestyle cultural thing that exists. Perhaps solutions can be devised to give them less barriers to confront.

S. Fattah: This is not a question. It's an observation in terms of the youth in institutions. We have found that the younger a person is when he becomes involved, the more likely he is to stay involved in institutions. In other words, in terms of his first exposure, maybe basically because he's neglected, but then once he goes in the Philadelphia Prison Study Center, he becomes acclimated to some other youths who begin to give him insight into the whole culture that scientists are talking about.

They also give him instructions into other types of survival techniques on the street. But even though he might be in the study center only about two months, when he comes out, he is a different person, he's turned on to something different, and so he goes into something different, and then he goes back to the study center, and it's like a revolving door.

The other comment I would make about rehabilitation is that in terms of dealing with young people, I think you're on safer ground not asking whether or not a person is guilty, because most of the young people seem to feel that everybody has done something wrong, they're just the ones who got caught. If you go along with that idea, you can deal with the youth. Perhaps, we should be dealing with them in terms of whatever goals they have set for themselves now, rather than going back over a whole pile of records and basing our judgment and future work on those records. Everybody seems to be a borderline deficient; I can't even remember all of the terminology, we don't pay too much attention to it. I think the best way to deal with that is not to say that anyone has done anything wrong, but to ask, "What are you going to do about the rest of your life?"

REFERENCES

1. Clifford R. Shaw and Henry D. McKay, *Juvenile Delinquency and Urban Areas* (Chicago: University of Chicago Press, 1942).

2. Gunnar Myrdal, *An American Dilemma* (New York: Harper & Row, 1944), p. 979.

3. Edwin H. Sutherland and Donald R. Cressey, *Criminology* (New York: J. B. Lippincott Company, 1970), p. 180.

4. David Abrahamsen, *The Psychology of Crime* (New York: The Macmillan Company, 1964), p. 104.

5. William F. Haddad and G. Douglas Pugh, *Black Economic Development* (Englewood Cliffs: Prentice-Hall, 1969), p. 9.

6. Richard D. Knudten, *Crime in a Complex Society: An Introduction to Criminology* (Homewood, Ill: The Dorsey Press, 1970), p. 71.

7. Richard R. Korn and Lloyd W. McCorkle, *Criminology and Penology* (New York: Holt, Rinehart and Winston, 1965), pp. 238-39.

8. *Ibid.,* p. 238.

9. Thomas F. Pettigrew, *A Profile of the Negro American* (New York: D. Van Nostrand Company, 1964), p. 138.

10. Stokely Carmichael and Charles Hamilton, *Black Power: The Politics of Liberation in America* (New York: Vintage Books, 1967), p. 4.

11. Louis L. Knowles and Kenneth Prewitt, eds., *Institutional Racism in America* (Englewood Cliffs, N.J.: Prentice-Hall, 1969), Ch. 1.

12. *Sonnets from the Portuguese,* Sonnet XLIII.

13. *See* D. A. Bell, Jr., "Racism in American Courts," *California Law Review,* 61 (Jan. 1973), 165-203; Knowles and Prewitt, *supra,* Ch. 5.

14. *Furman* v. *Georgia,* 408 U.S. 238 (1972); *Oyler* v. *Boles,* 368 U.S. 456 (1962) *(dictum)*; *Maxwell* v. *Bishop,* 398 F. 2d 138, 148 (8th Cir., 1968), vacated and remanded on other grounds, 398 U.S. 262 (1970); *Holt* v. *Hutto,* 363 F. Supp. 194 (D.D. Ar., 1973).

15. *Furman* v. *Georgia,* 408 U.S. 238.

16. Hubert M. Blalock, Jr., *Causal Inferences in Non-experimental Research* (New York: Norton, 1972), p. 13.

17. *Yick Wo* v. *Hopkins,* 118 U.S. 356 (1886).

18. Civil Rights Act of 1964, 42 U.S. Code Sec. 2000 *et. seq.,* as amended by the Equal Opportunity Act of 1972, USCA (Supp. 1973).

19. *Holt* v. *Hutto,* 363 F. Supp. 194.

20. *Ibid.,* at. p. 456.

21. *Williams* v. *New York,* 337 U.S. 241 (1949).

22. *See* Norval Morris, *The Future of Imprisonment* (Chicago: University of Chicago Press, 1974); American Friends Service Committee, *Struggle for Justice* (New York: Hill and Wang, 1971); Nicholas Kittrie, *The Right to be Different: Deviance and Enforced Therapy* (Baltimore: Penguin, 1974); Jessica Mitford, *Kind and Usual Punishment* (New York: Alfred Knopf, 1973).

23. "Effectiveness," as the term is used here and in most of the studies, means ability to reduce the rate of recidivism in ex-convicts.

24. Robert Martinson, "What Works?—Questions and Answers about Prison Reform," *The Public Interest,* 35 (1974), 22-45; James Robison and Gerald Smith, "The Effectiveness of Correctional Programs," *Crime and Delinquency* (17 Jan. 1971), 67-80.

25. Morris; American Friends Service Committee, *op. cit.,* footnote 304.

26. Norman A. Carlson, "Corrections—Past and Present," speech delivered to the North Virginia Association of Life Underwriters at Springfield, Virginia on February 13, 1975 (U.S. Dept. of Justice informational release); Carlson, "A Balanced Approach to Corrections," speech delivered to the Annual Conference of the National Sheriffs' Association at Memphis, Tennessee on June 17, 1975 (U.S. Dept. of Justice informational release).

27. "A Balanced Approach to Corrections," *supra,* pp. 7-9 (emphasis added).

28. President's Message to Congress, June 19, 1975.

29. *Time,* June 30, 1975, p. 22.

30. *The State* (Columbia, South Carolina), June 20, 1975, p. 2A, col. 1.

31. Press Release, "The Press Conference of Edward H. Levi, Attorney General of the United States," June 19, 1975, Office of the White House Press Secretary.

32. Official Press Release of the Office of the White House Press Secretary, New Haven, Connecticut, April 25, 1975.

Luncheon Speaker

Sterling Johnson

Thanks a lot Bob. It's nice seeing a lot of people I haven't seen in a long time.

It's an honor for me to be able to speak to you on a subject that is of fundamental concern to all who are present here today, and that is blacks in the criminal justice system.

When we talk of blacks in the criminal justice system, I'm reminded of one young black scholar who when asked how can blacks avoid the inequalities of the criminal justice system, he answered, "Don't get into it." The criminal justice system is so wrought with discrimination that we sometimes forget it.

Recently I had an occasion to have lunch with a friend. He was white and also a judge. I sat in the courtroom as he was concluding his morning business and what I noticed was fascinating. I noticed that the judge, district attorney, defense counsel, probation officers, court officers, policemen and court stenographers were white. I then took note of the prisoners who were being led in from the bullpen into the courtroom, and noticed that they were either all white, all black or Hispanic. This was our criminal justice system in action.

The only thing that blacks contributed to that system was defendants. As Richard Friar laments as far as the criminal justice system is concerned, talking about blacks, that's just what it is, "Just us."

As practitioners, you have observed or experienced the same thing, blacks are discriminated against, both as perpetrators and as victims. Statistics support the statement that there's a definite imbalance in the criminal justice system as it applies to blacks. First, blacks are over-represented as defendants. A recent U.S. Census Survey disclosed that although blacks represent only eleven percent of the nation's population, they represent over forty-seven percent of the prison population. The chance that a black will be arrested is four times that of a white person.

Moreover, blacks are more likely to be prosecuted than whites. It is no

161

secret that substantially more blacks are convicted after trial than are whites. If convicted, blacks are more likely to receive a stiffer sentence than whites.

For example, last month my office tried a twenty-two year old black addict for selling less than one-eighth of an ounce of heroin. There was a conviction. Two weeks ago, the defendant came before the judge for sentencing, and the judge said this, "I sentence you to jail for the rest of your natural life, the mandatory minimum sentence that you must serve before you are eligible for parole is one year. If this defendant is paroled on his first appearance, which I doubt will happen, he will be on parole for the rest of his natural life.

At the same time this event was taking place, directly across the street, in the federal courts in the Southern District of New York, a white rabbi admitted participating in a nursing home fraud. He had stolen millions of dollars from elderly residents and was being sentenced to four months imprisonment for this white collar crime. This man stole this money, and because of his greed, he forced thousands of elderly people to live in misery. Unlike the addict, this rabbi will not spend one day behind the cold, grey walls of a federal penitentiary.

I read in *The New York Times* on Thursday that the rabbi was ordered to serve his time in a halfway house on weekdays. He's gonna be home on the weekends. Later this sentence was altered to allow this man to begin his time in September after the summer months are over.

The inequities of the criminal justice system are not limited to offenders. While we are over-represented as the defendants of the system, we are grossly under-represented as prosecutors, judges, policemen, and probation officers. Inadequately represented as court reporters, defense counsel and in other policy-making positions. Today less than one percent of the nation's three hundred thousand lawyers are black. Clearly less than three thousand black lawyers in this our bicentennial year are totally unacceptable. Not only are blacks under-represented in the courts, they are seriously lacking in visibility on the nation's police forces; the traditional first encounter with the criminal justice system. It is surprising, though it should not be, that only 3.3 percent of all of the nation's police forces are black. Here in New York, it's estimated that the non-white population of the city is between thirty-five and forty percent, yet the police force in New York City is less than seven percent black. I think they have something like twenty-seven, twenty-eight thousand policemen, and you have less than two thousand black police officers here in New York City.

There have been approximately fifty police departments throughout the country, in recent years, that have been cited for their racial discriminatory policies. The federal agency that brought some of these actions and who is responsible to insure that these local departments do not discriminate in their hiring and promotions is the Justice Department. As Brother Malcolm would say, this is like asking the fox to watch the chickens.

The Drug Enforcement Administration which is charged with enforcing the federal narcotic laws has over twenty-two hundred agents stationed throughout the world. Of these, only one hundred and twenty-seven are black. Notwithstanding the drug problem in Harlem, Bedford-Stuyvesant, South Bronx and South Jamaica, there are less than twenty blacks assigned to the New York Office. And this is interesting because people quote five hundred thousand addicts and they also quote the fact that half of the drugs that are consumed and half of the trafficking in the United States exists right here in New York and yet there are less than twenty black federal DEA agents in New York City.

There are over ninety United States Attorneys in the nation. This is the chief federal prosecutors. None is black. In fact, of the thirty-four hundred attorneys working in the Justice Department, there are only one hundred and twelve or 3.3 percent who are black.

Currently, there are three hundred and seventy-seven active and one hundred and ten retired United States District Court Judges sitting in the United States. There are ninety-three active and forty-three retired Court of Appeal Judges sitting in the United States. Of these, more than six hundred federal judges, only five blacks sit on Appelate Courts and only fifteen sit in the District Courts. So that's twenty out of over six hundred federal judges.

You only have to look at these horrible statistics to realize that when it comes to blacks in the criminal justice system, we simply do not count.

Let us bring the microscope closer to home and look at the criminal justice system in a specific area in New York from a black perspective. In May of 1975, I was persuaded to return from Washington to be the City Special Narcotics Prosecutor. This was and is a very important job. I had the backing of the five district attorneys and I thought City Hall. How did the City receive me? Two months after I was sworn in, my budget was slashed from 2.4 million dollars to 1.3 million dollars. I cursed, I screamed, I pleaded, I told City Hall they had to be crazy, drug trafficking was increasing at an alarming rate and most of the traffic occurred in black neighborhoods. Pushers were fearless enough to put brand names on heroin and guarantee their products. They did everything, but advertise on radio or TV. My pleas fell on deaf ears.

Meanwhile, it was announced that the Democratic National Convention was to be held at Madison Square Garden. City Hall was determined to rid mid-Manhattan of prostitutes, a place where few blacks live. They formed what some referred to as a pussy posse. The posse arrested prostitutes, closed massage parlors and waged a relentless war on pornography. Meanwhile, uptown, where black folk live, the drug problem grew. Two or three hundred addicts would congregate on one corner strangling pedestrian traffic. The known brands of heroin increased from thirty-five last year to over two hundred this year.

Recently, a fifteen-year-old youth testified that he had a job of standing on a corner and just holding drugs for what they call scramblers, and he made five hundred dollars a week just holding drugs.

One dealer we arrested testified that he operated on one block, one block in Harlem and he made over fifty thousand dollars a week.

Budget time came around again and I related these same facts to City Hall. The results: The war on prostitution continues and the budget for my office was slashed from 1.3 million to 1.1 million. The bottom line is while the pussy posse continues to corral prostitutes, drug traffic in Harlem is so blatant that it's disgraceful. Even if the police were to make more arrests, the budget cuts make it almost impossible for proper prosecution of the cases in court.

A black police officer who operated as an undercover officer was laid off, had come into my office as I was preparing for a particular trial, and I asked him this question, "What or how would you define justice?" And he said, and I quote, "Justice is a statue in Foley Square that the pigeons shit on." When I am asked what I think of the criminal justice system as it relates to blacks, I can only reply, "For many many blacks there is no system, there is no justice, and it is criminal." Thank you.

REACTION

Woodson: Sterling, I'd like to pose a very obvious kind of question for response. You know we read in the paper about the contract that the Harlem drug dealers have on your life. Could you tell us about that?

Sterling: Well, I received a call one Saturday night and the police said they thought that I would be interested in speaking to a defendant they had just arrested. This defendant was arrested with two other individuals on a charge of possession of hand guns. One defendant admitted to two homicides where he had killed five people. He was a professional assassin, a professional hit man. Now we suspected him of committing forty other homicides.

So he gave us the name of the individual who was arranging the money for the contract on me and he also gave us the name of the individual who was recruiting the talent. I never heard of them, but the Police Department's Intelligence Division verified this.

It seems that there is a struggle going on in Harlem between the young drug pushers and the old drug pushers and the older drug pushers have to do something startling and eye-catching and appealing. They decided that they would have me "taken out" or assassinated because I have been very vocal and visible since I've come back to New York. Everytime I say something about drugs, and the police department feels pressure and they wipe the pushers off the streets and it brings a lot of pressure on the dealers in heroin, so they thought if they knocked me off, it would make the newspapers. The police gave me a guard around my house, accompanied my children to school, a walkie-talkie was given to my wife, and I had to wear a bullet-proof vest. A permit to carry a gun was also issued to me, but I don't wear the bullet-proof vest, it is too hot.

Commissioner Dunning: We very much talk about prison rights, very much talk about re-defining the whole concept of crime and criminology. And yet, as you stand here, you're one of the few prosecutors, possibly the only special prosecutor.

Would you comment on the ambivalent role that you play as a black prosecutor seeing what's happening in the black community with respect to drugs and guns, yet others are saying these youth are turning off because of society's negative impact?

Sterling: When it comes to drugs, the community wants to see drug pushers sent away for life. For those who are not New Yorkers, we have the toughest drug law in the nation. If you get caught selling an ounce or more of heroin, you must go away for a period of fifteen years and twenty-five years to life. There is no probation, there is no good time, no halfway house, and as soon as the jurors or the judge decide, or you plead guilty, it's off to prison. You receive no bail pending an appeal, and you must serve that mandatory minimum, fifteen years, before you're eligible for parole.

Now, after the fifteen years, they might let you out, but you're on parole for the rest of your life.

If you sell between an eighth of an ounce and an ounce of heroin, the period or the scope of punishment is between six and eight and a half years of life, and anything less than an ounce is one year to life.

It's been my experience that the law abiding citizens who are living on Eighth Avenue and 116th Street want drug pushers to go to jail for the rest of their lives.

A lot of people and a lot of penologists and a lot of criminologists have attacked this particular law. I don't think it's a good law myself. It has not stopped drug trafficking. The only thing that it has done is to insure that those who have been convicted of selling drugs do go to jail. In my experience, black people like to see drug pushers go to jail.

Last night we arrested a forty-year-old drug pusher, and what he was doing and what a lot of drug pushers are doing is employing kids and we arrested five or six sixteen and seventeen-year-old, very attractive, young girls, who we have what they call a "two-sales" on, and if convicted, these sixteen and seventeen-year-old kids must go away for life and a mandatory minimum of six to eight years. Community people were very angry at this older dope peddler, who was responsible for them being in their predicament.

Brooks: The Customs Department of the United States, as far as I know, only employs eighteen hundred people nationwide border to border so they can't be serious about drugs. Eighteen hundred people's luggage must go out of Kennedy every half hour, so they are not serious about reducing drug traffic; no one cares about drugs in the black community except mothers.

David Fattah: Re: Impact of socio-economic conditions on criminally motivated behavior.

Sterling: In this our bicentennial year, unemployment in Harlem and other black neighborhoods is as high as sixty percent. If I tell a black kid who's unemployed and whose parents are under-employed, that he should study and work hard and be a contributing citizen, he would look at me and say, "Nigger, you got to be crazy!" His hero is the guy who is driving the Mercedes, who's got the Cadillac, the Mark IV, who's got two or three thousand dollars on a schoolyard basketball game up in Harlem. So the temptation to engage in criminal activities is too great, and the money is there to be made.

Lamb: There are some people who seem to think that if you take the profit out of drugs, it would have an impact on the amount of sales. What are your thoughts?

Sterling: That's a very simple answer to a very complex problem. Let's take a look at methadone maintenance programs as an example. Methadone has been given out for years and what has been the result? One of the biggest problems with methadone is the diversion. People are just selling methadone. Taking the profit out of it is not the answer, and I don't think there is any one answer. I think it goes back to jobs, housing, education. You have to have adequate enforcement, prosecution, but most important there has to be a commitment from the White House and a commitment from City Hall and resources.
President Ford gave his speech about drugs. All he said was there should be mandatory minimum sentences to confront the drug problem. The only thing that is going to insure us is that if a person is convicted they are going to jail. But as far as New York is concerned, since we have that

mandatory minimum sentence, there are more addicts, more pushers and more dealers.

Dunning: Do you believe in rehabilitation programs? Should more money be put into them?

Sterling: Yes! One of the things that the Mayor of New York did was not only to slash my budget, but he decimated the rehabilitation programs. It is estimated that thirty thousand addicts will be back on the streets once they are released from prison.

Fattah: How many major drug suppliers would you say there are and how much are they getting out of it?

Sterling: There is really no one major supply. In the recent past, black drug peddlers would have to go through station organized crime figures to get their drugs to sell. But with the Vietnam War, the blacks got very sophisticated. They do not need the Italian connection to sell their drugs. They have their own connections over in Southeast Asia.

Now what they have done is to go to Southeast Asia, establish a connection over there, buy a kilo for three thousand dollars and pay a couple of servicemen some money to smuggle it in when they come back. These black dealers in turn sell this kilo for thirty, forty thousand dollars. Now, blacks are now in it from what they call the womb to the tomb. When the drug dealers receive the shipment, they will cut it up, step on it and make ten kilos out of one kilo and they will give it to their workers and they in turn will sell the drugs fifty-five dollars a quarter. So blacks are into drug trafficking from the importation level all the way down to the distribution level.

The old time what they used to have is one guy who would import it, he'd sell it to a middle-level dealer. Another guy would cut it up and sell it to somebody else. Blacks would get in it, get a load and they'd get out. But now blacks are getting in it and staying with it all the way.

There is more money in it that way, but there's also more risk.

Now, there is no one monolithic structure in the drug traffic. You've got a lot of independents; there is room for everybody. I couldn't answer the question how many big pushers there are because as soon as we take one off, there's somebody else to take his place.

I'm going to be making some arrests and some indictments in the near future, and as soon as I do that, it's just like a baseball team—one guy gets hurt, or a football team, one guy gets hurt you take him off the field and put somebody else in. And they have more resources and more commitments than the law enforcement authorities have.

At one time, the Mexican heroin represented only ten percent of the national market, and that market was confined to along the southwest border and in California. And when Nixon, for political reasons, waged a war on drugs, and he got Turkey to stop growing the opium poppy, this dried up a particular source. For a time, we were patting ourselves on the backs saying we've turned the corner on the war on drugs. The Mexican heroin moved into this particular vacuum, whereas eighty percent of the heroin that's consumed in the United States right now is the Mexican brown heroin.

Now, interesting enough, we've got these places that I mentioned, Harlem, South Bronx, South Jamaica and Bedford-Stuyvesant. These are where your black people live and for some reason, blacks prefer white heroin from Southeast Asia. In the East Village, that is predominately white, they prefer the dark heroin. Whites prefer the dark and blacks prefer the white. The reason? I don't know.

I refer to the heroin makers who produce the Mexican heroin as the short-order cooks, and the people who make the French or the Southeast Asia heroin as the chefs. You get a package of Mexican heroin that's forty percent, you've got a good package. If you've got a package of Southeast Asia or European heroin that's ninety-five to ninety-nine percent, that's good heroin. In fact, in Europe, they had one fellow who had something like ten kilos that was eighty-two percent, and he was so ashamed of that he wouldn't even put that out on the market.

Summary

Robert L. Woodson

The importance of a major symposium such as this is reflected in the far reaching effect that its activities can have in bringing about change within the criminal justice system. The symposium participants were undoubtedly among the highest qualified practitioners within the field, and their position and respect in the profession are noteworthy. It is this fact that has motivated the National Urban League to press for expanded utilization of black researchers, criminologists and criminal justice practitioners by federal, state and local agencies, in a collective effort in the war against crime.

Research has consistently played a role in the allocation and distribution of funds within the criminal justice field, if not directly through specific empirical findings then by the influencing of public opinion. Many non-minority researchers are identified by the media as being the leading authorities and thus they are called upon to offer commentary on a variety of topics, even when they possess no special knowledge on the subject at hand. Unfortunately the majority of research being conducted is being done by middle and upper-class whites, and their interpretation of the data is influenced by their backgrounds. Therefore, in order to overcome this limitation, there is a need to utilize black and other minority researchers and criminologists, whose kinship and sensitivity brings them closer to the problems of the black and minority community. In addition, their academic skills make them the best qualified to assist in the fight against crime. However, the mere substitution of the views of white middle-class academic opinion with the views of black academicians, unto itself will fail to produce sound, useful policy.

The participation of a broad cross-section of minority criminal justice practitioners, as well as lay citizens who are most affected by the crime problem will add immeasurably to the quality of the results. For too long such input has been ignored by researchers and policy makers. Only with the cross-fertilization of ideas and experiences of the academic, professional and lay people can meaningful public policy be produced.

169

Policy developed from the top levels of public and private bureaucratic life has failed to produce solutions to the major social ills of society. People residing in local neighborhoods have, over the years, successfully addressed a full range of social problems. However, many of these efforts go largely ignored by policy-makers, who cling doggedly to approaches that are of limited vision and thus have failed to deliver. Social policy "experts" tend to look exclusively to one another for answers.

It was the consensus of the symposium participants that new formulas must be devised in pursuing solutions to urban crime. A careful assessment must be made of those neighborhood crime prevention programs which have been successful, with an eye toward singling out the specific aspects which directly attribute to the programs' success. If indeed it is the local residents who have the clearest understanding and capacity to address the wide range of social discomforts, then public policy should be in the position of assisting those residents in their struggle rather than bureaucratically administering undermining local efforts. Public policy should come directly from the people, in some cases instigated by those closest to the problem.

All people want the incidence of crime slashed drastically. It is because of this that people want realistic programs instituted to cut crime and halt urban blight. We cannot afford the luxury of fake solutions to the problem; pseudo solutions that promise but do not deliver. People who are most traumatized by these conditions are beginning to demand an accounting from those charged with controlling the resources that can influence solutions.

These people are beginning to understand that they have no permanent friends or permanent enemies, just permanent issues. To the extent that those of us in policy development understand and relate to that reality, will be the extent to which we will be allowed to play any role in finding solutions.

List of Attendees

Mr. Robert Barr
Detective
Newark Police Department
22 Franklin Street
Newark, NJ
(202) 733-6007

Mr. John Boone
Director of Urban Affairs
Station WNAC-TV
RKO General Corporation
Boston, MA
(617) 725-2758

Ms. Geraldine Brooks
Education Coordinator
National Urban Coalition
1201 Connecticut Avenue, NW
Washington, DC
(202) 331-2400

Dr. Lee P. Brown
Director of Justice Services
Multnomah County Court House
Room 809
Portland, OR
(503) 248-3701

Mr Ronald H. Brown
Deputy Executive Director of

Programs & Government Affairs
National Urban League
500 East 62nd Street
New York, NY 10021
(212) 644-6531

Mr. Herrington Bryce
Director of Research
Joint Center for Political Studies
1426 H Street, NW
Washington, DC
(202) 638-4477

Dr. Benjamin Carmichael
Associate Professor
California State University
Hayward, CA 94611

Mr. Cornelius Cooper
Regional Administrator
Law Enforcement Assistance Admin.
325 Chestnut Street
Philadelphia, PA
(215) 983-5574

Ms. Jacqueline Corbett
Senior Social Researcher
National Center for Juvenile Justice
3409 Forbes Avenue
Pittsburgh, PA 15260
(412) 624-6104

171

Dr. Ronald Davenport
Dean
Duquesne University School
   of Law
600 Forbes Avenue
Pittsburgh, PA 15219
(412) 434-6280

Mr. Roosevelt Dunning
Deputy Commissioner
New York City Police Department
1 Police Plaza
New York, NY 10038
(212) 374-5323

Mr. William E. Dye
Chief of Police
Champaign Police Department
14 E. University Avenue
Champaign, IL 61820

Mr. James Dyer
Program Officer
Carnegie Corporation
437 Madison Avenue
New York, NY 10022

Mr. Chaka Fattah
Assistant Director
House of Umoja
1444 N. Frazier Street
Philadelphia, PA 19134

Sister Falaka Fattah
House of Umoja
1436 N. Frazier Street
Philadelphia, PA 19134
(215) 473-9978

Mr. Hassan Fattah
Counselor
House of Umoja
1442 N. Frazier Street
Philadelphia, PA 19134
(215) 473-9978

Mr. Sharif Fattah
Staff Counselor
House of Umoja
1442 N. Frazier Street
Philadelphia, PA 19134
(215) 473-9978

Ms. Barbara Garrey
Editor
G. K. Hall & Company
70 Lincoln Street
Boston, MA 02111
(617) 423-3990

Mr. James Hargrove
Chairman, Region #1
National Black Police Association
290 East 56th Street
Brooklyn, NY 11203
(212) 495-6265

Ms. Elfreda Howard
121-17 Grayson Street
Springfield Gardens, NY 11413

Mr. Sterling Johnson
Special Narcotics Prosecutor
City of New York
New York, NY
(212) 577-1218-19

Ms. Rosetta Kerr
Director of Youth Diversion Program
Baltimore Urban League
1102 Mondawmin Concourse
Baltimore, MD 21215
(301) 728-5515

Mr. Robert Lamb
Regional Director
Community Relations Service
U.S. Department of Justice
915 2nd Street
Seattle, WA 98174
(206) 442-4465

Dr. George W. Logan
Assistant Professor
Michigan State University
East Lansing, MI
(517) 353-4759

Mrs. Merlissie Middleton
Chairman
Department of Sociology
Morris Brown College
643 Hunter Street, NW
Atlanta, GA 30314
(404) 525-7831

Mr. Archibald Murray
Attorney-in-Chief & Executive
  Director
Legal Aid Society
15 Park Row
New York, NY 10038
(212) 577-3313

Dr. George Napper
Director, Crime Analysis Team
Division of the Mayor's Office
96 Mitchell Street, NW
Atlanta, GA 30303

Ms. Diane R. Palm
Board Member
Community Assistance Project
150 West 5th Street
Chester, PA
(215) 876-5571

Dr. Gwynne Peirson
Professor of Criminology
Department of Sociology &
  Anthropology
Howard University
Washington, DC
(202) 636-6853

Ms. Ruby Ryles
Associate Director of Public
  Relations
New York Director of Public
  Correctional Services
State Office Campus #2
Albany, NY 12226
(518) 457-8182

Dr. Andrea D. Sullivan
Director
Crime Prevention Project
National Urban League
500 East 62nd Street
New York, NY 10021
(212) 644-6440-1-2

Ms. Cynthia Sulton
Police Foundation
1909 K Street, NW
Washington, DC 20006
(202) 833-1640

Dr. Llewellyn Alex Swan
Professor & Chairman
Department of Sociology
Fisk University
Nashville, TN 37203
(615) 329-9111 Ext. 216-278

Mr. Lew Taylor
Special Assistant
Office of the Administrator
Law Enforcement Assistance Admin.
633 Indiana Avenue, NW
Washington, DC 20531
(202) 376-3936

Mr. George Thomas
National Black Police Association
130 Chancellor Avenue
Newark, NJ
(201) 733-6135

Ms. Peggy Triplett
Special Assistant to the Director
National Institute for Law
  Enforcement & Criminal Justice
Law Enforcement Assistance
  Admin.
633 Indiana Avenue, NW
Washington, DC 20531
(202) 376-3606

Dr. Wyatt Tee Walker
Pastor
Canaan Baptist Church
132 West 116th Street
New York, NY
(212) 866-0301

Commissioner Benjamin Ward
N.Y. State Department of
  Correctional Services
State Office Campus, Bldg. #2
Albany, NY 14226
(518) 457-8134

Mr. Hubert Williams
Police Director
Newark Police Department
Newark, NJ
(201) 733-6007

Dr. James Q. Wilson
Professor of Goverment
Harvard University
Cambridge, MA 02138
(617) 495-2150

Robert L. Woodson
Fellow in Residence
American Enterprise
  Institute
1150 17th Street
Washington, D.C. 20036
(202) 296-5616

THE LIBRARY
ST. MARY'S COLLEGE OF MARYLAND
ST. MARY'S CITY, MARYLAND 20686

087309